The Psychology of Entrepreneurship

Mastering the Mindset of Successful Entrepreneurs and Applying It to Grow Your Business

Shawn Barrett

ISBN: 979-8874225117

CONTENTS

INTRODUCTION

Welcome to a journey that will transform your life. This book is your guide to becoming an entrepreneur who thrives, not just survives. Here, you'll find the tools, insights, and motivation to turn your dreams into reality. Let's dive into what you can expect and how this book will change you.

Entrepreneurship is more than starting a business. It’s about embracing a mindset that sees opportunities where others see obstacles. By the end of this book, you will have developed this mindset. You will learn to think like an entrepreneur, act with purpose, and overcome challenges with confidence.

This book is structured to build your entrepreneurial mindset step by step. Each chapter focuses on a different trait or skill that successful entrepreneurs share. From creativity to resilience, risk-taking to vision, you will gain a deep understanding of what it takes to succeed. More importantly, you will learn how to apply these traits in your own life.

Expect to be challenged. The exercises and reflections in this book are designed to push you out of your comfort zone. Growth happens when you stretch beyond what you thought possible. By engaging fully with the content, you will develop new habits and ways of thinking that will serve you for life.

You will also be inspired. Throughout the book, you'll read stories of entrepreneurs who have overcome incredible odds. These real-world examples will show you that success is possible, no matter where you start or what obstacles you face. Their journeys will motivate you to keep going, even when things get tough.

Here's how this book will change you:

Increased Creativity

You will learn to see connections where others see none. Creativity is about more than just having new ideas; it's about seeing the world differently. This book will teach you techniques to enhance your creative thinking and apply it to solve problems in innovative ways.

Greater Resilience

Setbacks are inevitable in any entrepreneurial journey. This book will help you build resilience so that you can bounce back stronger from any failure. You will learn to view challenges as opportunities for growth and to keep pushing forward no matter what.

Enhanced Risk-Taking

Taking risks is essential for growth. This book will teach you how to take calculated risks that can lead to big rewards. You will learn to assess potential risks and make informed decisions that align with your goals.

Clear Vision

Vision is what keeps you focused and motivated. This book will guide you in crafting a clear and compelling vision for your future. You will learn to set long-term goals and develop a plan to achieve them. Your vision will become the driving force behind everything you do.

Practical Skills

Beyond mindset, this book offers practical skills you can apply immediately. From networking to time management, you will learn techniques that will make you more effective in your daily life. These skills are the foundation of entrepreneurial success.

As you work through this book, you will start to notice changes in your thinking and behavior. You will become more proactive, seeking out opportunities instead of waiting for them to come to you. You will develop a stronger belief in your abilities and a clearer sense of purpose. By the end of this journey, you will be ready to take on any challenge and turn your dreams into reality.

This book is not just about reading; it's about doing. Each chapter includes exercises and reflections designed to help you apply what you've learned. Take the time to complete these activities fully. They are the key to transforming your mindset and developing the habits that lead to success.

Remember, every successful entrepreneur started with a dream. They faced challenges, made mistakes, and kept going. This book will show you that you can do the same. You have everything you need to succeed within you. All it takes is the right mindset, the willingness to learn, and the courage to take action.

Welcome to your entrepreneurial journey. Let's get started and make your dreams a reality.

CHAPTER 1

TRAITS EVERY ENTREPRENEUR NEEDS TO SUCCEED

Understanding the entrepreneurial mindset is essential for anyone looking to succeed in business. This mindset is a blend of traits that help entrepreneurs see opportunities, take risks, and overcome challenges.

In this chapter, we will explore these key traits and how they contribute to entrepreneurial success. By understanding and developing these traits, you can enhance your own entrepreneurial journey.

An entrepreneurial mindset is about more than just starting a business. It's about thinking differently and acting decisively. It involves a unique combination of attitudes and skills that empower individuals to turn ideas into reality. Developing this mindset can make a significant difference, whether you're launching a startup or driving innovation within an existing organization.

Defining the Entrepreneurial Mindset

Picture an entrepreneur. What do you see? Maybe someone who is always coming up with new ideas or a person who doesn't give up easily. These are just some parts of the entrepreneurial mindset. This mindset is like a toolkit filled with creativity, resilience, risk-taking, and vision.

An entrepreneurial mindset is more than just thinking about business. It's a way of seeing the world and solving problems. Entrepreneurs are people who don't settle for the way things are. They imagine how things could be better and work to make that vision a reality. This mindset involves looking at obstacles as opportunities, not as barriers.

One important aspect of the entrepreneurial mindset is the ability to stay positive in the face of setbacks. Entrepreneurs understand that failure is a part of the process and not the end. They use their failures as learning experiences to improve and try again. This positive outlook helps them to keep moving forward even when things get tough.

Another key part of the entrepreneurial mindset is adaptability. The business world is constantly changing, and entrepreneurs need to be able to change with it. This means being open to new ideas and willing to pivot when necessary. Flexibility and adaptability are crucial for staying relevant and successful in a competitive market.

Creativity: Connecting the Dots

Creativity is more than just having new ideas. It's about seeing connections that others miss. Entrepreneurs often find new uses for old things or come up with unique solutions to problems. For example, imagine looking at a pile of scrap metal and seeing the potential for a sculpture. Entrepreneurs thrive by creating new paths in the marketplace.

Creativity in entrepreneurship involves thinking outside the box. It's about finding innovative solutions to problems and coming up with new ways to do things. This can mean developing a new product, finding a better way to deliver a service, or creating a new market. Entrepreneurs who are creative can see possibilities that others miss.

A great example of creativity in entrepreneurship is the story of Airbnb. The founders, Brian Chesky and Joe Gebbia, saw an opportunity where others saw none. During a design conference in San Francisco, they noticed that all the hotels were booked. They decided to rent out air mattresses in their apartment to conference attendees. This simple idea grew into a global business that revolutionized the hospitality industry.

Creativity is not just about having ideas but about implementing them. It's about taking action and bringing those ideas to life. Entrepreneurs who can turn their creative ideas into reality have a significant advantage in the marketplace.

Developing creativity involves practice and a willingness to experiment. Here are some practical tips to enhance your creativity:

Keep a journal of ideas

Write down every idea that comes to mind, no matter how small or impractical it seems. Reviewing your journal regularly can spark new connections and insights.

Try new things

Step out of your comfort zone and explore different activities and experiences. This can help you see things from different perspectives.

Collaborate with others

Working with people from different backgrounds and industries can provide fresh ideas and viewpoints.

Take breaks

Sometimes stepping away from a problem can help you see it more clearly. Taking breaks can refresh your mind and boost creativity.

Stay curious

Always ask questions and seek to learn more. Curiosity can lead to new insights and ideas.

RESILIENCE: BOUNCING BACK STRONGER

Resilience is the ability to keep going after facing failure. Entrepreneurs know that failure is part of the process. Instead of seeing failure as the end, they view it as a chance to learn and improve. Think of resilience as the ability to get back up after falling, ready to try again. This quality is as crucial to an entrepreneur as oxygen is to fire.

Being resilient means not giving up when things get tough. It's about having the determination to push through obstacles and keep working towards your goals. This mindset is essential for entrepreneurs, as the journey is often filled with challenges and setbacks. Successful entrepreneurs are those who can stay focused and keep moving forward, no matter what.

One example of resilience in entrepreneurship is the story of J.K. Rowling. Before she became famous for writing the Harry Potter series, she faced numerous rejections from publishers. Instead of giving up, she continued to believe in her work and kept submitting her manuscript. Her persistence paid off, and today, she is one of the most successful authors in the world.

Developing resilience involves building mental and emotional strength. Here are some practical tips to enhance your resilience:

Reflect on past failures
Take time to think about your past failures and what you learned from them. This can help you see failure as a learning opportunity rather than a setback.

Set realistic goals
Break your long-term goals into smaller, achievable steps. This can help you stay motivated and focused on making progress.

Seek support
Surround yourself with people who encourage and support you. Having a strong support network can provide the emotional strength needed to overcome challenges.

Practice self-care

Taking care of your physical and mental health is crucial for building resilience. Make sure to get enough rest, eat well, and engage in activities that help you relax and recharge.

Stay positive

Maintain a positive outlook and focus on your strengths. Positive thinking can help you stay motivated and resilient.

RISK-TAKING: CALCULATED DECISIONS

Taking risks is another important trait. But it's not about gambling. Entrepreneurs assess situations, weigh the pros and cons, and then decide. They know that rewards often come from stepping into the unknown. This doesn't mean being reckless. It means making informed decisions even when the outcome is uncertain.

Risk-taking is a crucial part of entrepreneurship. Without taking risks, it's hard to achieve significant success. However, successful entrepreneurs know how to manage risks effectively. They don't take unnecessary risks but make calculated decisions based on thorough research and analysis.

A well-known example of risk-taking in entrepreneurship is Elon Musk. He took significant risks by investing in SpaceX and Tesla, ventures that many believed would fail. Despite numerous challenges and setbacks, his calculated risks paid off, and both companies are now industry leaders.

Developing the ability to take calculated risks involves several key steps:

Research and gather information

Before making a decision, gather as much information as possible. This includes understanding the market, potential challenges, and opportunities.

Evaluate the pros and cons

Carefully weigh the potential benefits and drawbacks of each decision. Consider the worst-case scenario and how you would handle it.

Start small

Begin by taking smaller risks to build your confidence. As you become more comfortable with risk-taking, you can gradually take on bigger challenges.

Learn from others

Study the experiences of successful entrepreneurs and learn from their risk-taking strategies. This can provide valuable insights and inspiration.

Be prepared to pivot

If things don't go as planned, be ready to change direction. Flexibility and adaptability are key to managing risks effectively.

Taking calculated risks involves being prepared for the unexpected. Entrepreneurs need to be adaptable and ready to pivot if things don't go as planned. This flexibility allows them to navigate uncertainty and seize opportunities that others might miss.

VISION: GUIDING THE WAY

Vision is what guides entrepreneurs through tough times. It's more than just a goal. Vision is a clear picture of what the future could be. Entrepreneurs use their vision to inspire themselves and others. This vision helps them stay focused and motivated, even when challenges arise.

Having a strong vision is essential for entrepreneurial success. It provides direction and purpose, helping entrepreneurs stay on course even when faced with obstacles. A clear vision allows entrepreneurs to see beyond the present and imagine what their business can achieve in the future.

A great example of vision in entrepreneurship is Walt Disney. He had a clear vision of creating a magical place where families could enjoy entertainment together. Despite facing numerous challenges, including financial difficulties and skepticism, he remained committed to his vision. Today, Disney is a global entertainment empire that continues to bring joy to millions of people.

Developing a strong vision involves several key steps:

Define your goals

Clearly articulate what you want to achieve in the long term. Your vision should be specific, measurable, and inspiring.

Write it down

Put your vision in writing and keep it visible. This serves as a constant reminder of what you're working towards.

Share your vision

Communicate your vision with your team and stakeholders. A shared vision can inspire and motivate everyone involved.

Review and refine

Regularly review your vision and make adjustments as needed. This ensures that your vision remains relevant and achievable.

Stay committed

Even when faced with challenges, stay focused on your vision. Commitment to your vision helps you navigate obstacles and stay motivated.

A strong vision not only guides the entrepreneur but also inspires others to join the journey. It creates a sense of purpose and direction, making it easier to navigate challenges and stay focused on long-term goals.

How These Traits Work Together

These traits don't work alone. They interact and support each other. Creativity sparks new ideas. Vision provides direction. Risk-taking moves the process forward. Resilience ensures that setbacks are just temporary obstacles. Together, they form a powerful mindset that drives success.

Understanding how these traits interact is key to developing a strong entrepreneurial mindset. For example, creativity without vision can lead to scattered efforts. Vision without resilience can crumble at the first sign of failure. Risk-taking without creativity can result in missed opportunities.

By developing a balanced set of traits, entrepreneurs can create a robust foundation for their business. This involves not only honing each trait individually but also understanding how they complement and reinforce each other.

Tips for Developing These Traits

Creativity

Keep a journal of ideas. Try to connect unrelated concepts.

Resilience

Reflect on past failures and what you learned from them.

Risk-Taking

Start by taking small, calculated risks. Gradually increase as you become more comfortable.

Vision

Write down your long-term goals. Keep them visible to stay motivated.

Seek feedback

Regularly ask for feedback on your ideas and plans. This can provide new perspectives and help you improve.

Stay flexible

Be open to change and willing to pivot when necessary. Flexibility is key to adapting to new challenges and opportunities.

These tips provide practical steps for developing each trait. By incorporating these practices into your daily routine, you can strengthen your entrepreneurial mindset and increase your chances of success.

Real-World Examples

Consider Steve Jobs, co-founder of Apple. His creativity and vision revolutionized technology. He took calculated risks and bounced back from failures, like when he was initially ousted from Apple. His mindset exemplifies how these traits can lead to extraordinary success.

Another example is Oprah Winfrey. Her resilience and vision helped her overcome significant personal and professional challenges. She took risks in starting her own network and remained committed to her vision of creating meaningful content. Her journey shows how these traits can work together to achieve remarkable success.

People like Steve Jobs and Oprah Winfrey show how these traits work in practice. They provide inspiration and proof that developing an entrepreneurial mindset can lead to significant achievements. Studying the experiences of successful entrepreneurs can offer valuable insights and motivation.

Conclusion

The entrepreneurial mindset is a blend of creativity, resilience, risk-taking, and vision. These traits help entrepreneurs navigate challenges and seize opportunities. By developing these traits, you can strengthen your own entrepreneurial journey. In the next chapter, we will explore how emotional intelligence enhances these traits and contributes to success.

CHAPTER 2

THE HIDDEN TOOL EVERY ENTREPRENEUR USES TO SUCCEED

Emotional intelligence (EI) is a crucial skill for entrepreneurs. It helps them navigate the complex world of business by managing their own emotions and understanding others. This chapter explores the different dimensions of EI and how they contribute to entrepreneurial success. By developing these skills, entrepreneurs can enhance their leadership, decision-making, and relationships.

In business, success often hinges on effective communication and strong relationships. EI provides the tools to understand and manage emotions, making it easier to connect with others. This chapter will delve into the key components of EI, offering practical tips and real-world examples to help you apply these concepts in your entrepreneurial journey.

UNDERSTANDING EMOTIONAL INTELLIGENCE

Emotional intelligence is the ability to understand and manage your own emotions while recognizing and influencing the emotions of others. This skill is vital for entrepreneurs because business is not just about numbers, it's also about people. EI helps entrepreneurs build strong relationships, handle stress, and make better decisions.

There are five key dimensions of EI: self-awareness, self-regulation, empathy, social skills, and motivation. Each of these plays a critical role in entrepreneurial success. Together, they help entrepreneurs lead their teams effectively, connect with customers, and navigate the ups and downs of running a business.

Self-awareness is the foundation of EI. It involves recognizing your emotions and understanding how they affect your thoughts and actions. Entrepreneurs who are self-aware can manage their reactions and make decisions that align with their values and goals.

Self-regulation is the ability to control your emotions and behaviors. It means staying calm under pressure and avoiding impulsive decisions. Entrepreneurs who can regulate their emotions are better equipped to handle stress and make thoughtful decisions.

Empathy is the ability to understand and share the feelings of others. It helps entrepreneurs connect with their team, customers, and partners. By being empathetic, entrepreneurs can build strong relationships and create a positive work environment.

Social skills are the ability to interact effectively with others. This includes communication, conflict resolution, and teamwork. Entrepreneurs with strong social skills can build and lead effective teams, negotiate successfully, and create positive relationships with customers and partners.

Motivation is the drive to achieve your goals. It involves setting and working towards long-term objectives. Entrepreneurs who are motivated are passionate about their work and inspire others to share their vision.

Self-Awareness, Knowing Yourself

Self-awareness is the foundation of EI. It involves understanding your own emotions, strengths, weaknesses, and values. Entrepreneurs who are self-aware can manage their reactions and make decisions that align with their values and goals.

Being self-aware means knowing what triggers your emotions and how those emotions impact your behavior. For example, if you know that stress makes you short-tempered, you can take steps to manage your stress before it affects your interactions with others.

Self-awareness also involves understanding your strengths and weaknesses. Knowing what you are good at can help you leverage your skills and delegate tasks that you are less suited for. This can improve your efficiency and effectiveness as an entrepreneur.

Additionally, self-awareness helps you align your actions with your values. When you are clear about what matters most to you, it is easier to make decisions that are consistent with your long-term goals. This alignment can increase your sense of fulfillment and purpose in your work.

Finally, self-awareness enables you to understand the impact of your behavior on others. By being mindful of how your actions affect your team, you can create a more positive and productive work environment. This can lead to better collaboration and higher morale within your organization.

Tips for Developing Self-Awareness

Developing self-awareness involves regular self-reflection and seeking feedback from others. Here are some practical tips:

Keep a journal
Set aside time each day or week to reflect on your experiences and emotions. Write about your thoughts and feelings. This can help you recognize patterns and triggers in your emotions.

Ask for feedback
Seek honest feedback from trusted colleagues and mentors. Talking to people with different viewpoints can provide valuable insights into how others perceive you.

Practice mindfulness
Mindfulness techniques, like meditation, can help you stay present and aware of your emotions.

Set personal goals

Identify areas for improvement and set specific goals to enhance your self-awareness.

By developing self-awareness, you can better understand yourself and how you interact with the world. This understanding is crucial for effective leadership and decision-making in entrepreneurship.

SELF-REGULATION: MANAGING YOUR EMOTIONS

Self-regulation is the ability to control your emotions and behaviors. It means staying calm under pressure and avoiding impulsive decisions. Entrepreneurs who can regulate their emotions are better equipped to handle stress and make thoughtful decisions.

Self-regulation involves managing your emotional responses, especially in challenging situations. For example, if a deal falls through, instead of reacting with anger or frustration, a self-regulated entrepreneur will take a moment to calm down and think through the next steps.

Self-regulation also involves being adaptable. Entrepreneurs often face unexpected challenges and changes. Being able to adjust your plans and actions in response to new information is crucial for success. Flexibility allows you to stay on course even when circumstances change.

Additionally, self-regulation helps you maintain a professional demeanor. In business, how you present yourself can significantly impact your success. By controlling your emotions, you can ensure that you respond to situations in a composed and rational manner. This can build trust and respect with your team, customers, and partners.

Moreover, self-regulation can enhance your decision-making process. Emotions can cloud judgment and lead to impulsive decisions. By managing your emotions, you can approach decisions with a clear and rational mindset. This can improve the quality of your decisions and lead to better outcomes for your business.

TIPS FOR IMPROVING SELF-REGULATION

Pause before reacting

When you feel a strong emotion, take a moment to pause and breathe. This can prevent impulsive reactions.

Develop healthy coping strategies

Exercise, hobbies, and relaxation techniques can help you manage stress and maintain emotional balance.

Set clear goals and boundaries

Having clear goals and boundaries can help you stay focused and avoid emotional burnout.

Create a routine

Having a daily routine can help you stay organized and reduce stress.

Avoid triggers

Identify and minimize exposure to situations or people that trigger negative emotions.

By developing self-regulation, you can manage your emotions effectively and respond to challenges with a clear and composed mindset. This skill is essential for navigating the ups and downs of entrepreneurship.

EMPATHY: UNDERSTANDING OTHERS

Empathy is the ability to understand and share the feelings of others. It helps entrepreneurs connect with their team, customers, and partners. By being empathetic, entrepreneurs can build strong relationships and create a positive work environment.

Empathy involves listening actively and putting yourself in others' shoes. For example, if a team member is struggling with a task, an empathetic entrepreneur would take the time to understand their challenges and offer support.

Empathy also involves being aware of non-verbal cues. Body language, facial expressions, and tone of voice can provide important information about how someone is feeling. By paying attention to these cues, you can gain a deeper understanding of their emotions.

Additionally, empathy helps you build trust and rapport with others. When people feel understood and valued, they are more likely to be open and cooperative. This can lead to stronger relationships and better collaboration within your team.

Moreover, empathy can enhance your customer relationships. Understanding your customers' needs and emotions can help you create products and services that truly meet their needs. This can increase customer satisfaction and loyalty, which are crucial for business success.

Tips for Developing Empathy

Listen actively

Pay attention to what others are saying without interrupting. Show that you value their perspective.

Ask open-ended questions

Encourage others to share their thoughts and feelings by asking questions that require more than a yes or no answer.

Practice perspective-taking

Try to see situations from others' points of view. This can help you understand their emotions and motivations.

Practice active listening

Focus on the speaker and avoid distractions.

Reflect on your own emotions

Understanding your own emotions can help you relate to others.

By developing empathy, you can better understand and connect with others. This skill is essential for building strong relationships and creating a positive work environment.

Social Skills & Building Relationships

Social skills are the ability to interact effectively with others. This includes communication, conflict resolution, and teamwork. Entrepreneurs with strong social skills can build and lead effective teams, negotiate successfully, and create positive relationships with customers and partners.

Good social skills involve clear communication and active listening. For example, when leading a meeting, an entrepreneur with strong social skills would ensure everyone has a chance to speak and that their input is valued.

Social skills also involve being persuasive. Entrepreneurs often need to convince others to support their ideas or invest in their business. Being able to communicate your vision clearly and persuasively can help you gain buy-in from stakeholders.

Additionally, social skills help you build a positive work environment. By fostering open communication and encouraging teamwork, you can create a culture of collaboration and mutual respect. This can lead to higher morale and productivity within your organization.

Moreover, strong social skills can enhance your networking abilities. Building a broad network of contacts can provide valuable resources and opportunities for your business. By cultivating positive relationships with industry peers, mentors, and potential partners, you can expand your reach and influence.

Tips for Enhancing Social Skills

Here are some tips to enhance social skills:

Communicate clearly

Be clear and concise in your communication. Make sure your message is understood.

Build rapport

Take the time to get to know your team members and colleagues. Building rapport can strengthen relationships and improve collaboration.

Resolve conflicts effectively

Address conflicts directly and constructively. Focus on finding solutions rather than assigning blame.

Practice active listening

Show that you are engaged in the conversation by nodding, making eye contact, and summarizing what the other person has said.

Be approachable

Smile, make eye contact, and use open body language to make others feel comfortable around you.

Develop your negotiation skills

Learn techniques for effective negotiation and practice them in various situations.

By developing social skills, you can interact effectively with others and build strong, positive relationships. This skill is essential for leading teams and creating a collaborative work environment.

MOTIVATION, DRIVING YOURSELF AND OTHERS

Motivation is the drive to achieve your goals. It involves setting and working towards long-term objectives. Entrepreneurs who are motivated are passionate about their work and inspire others to share their vision.

Motivation is about having a clear purpose and staying committed to it. For example, an entrepreneur who is motivated by a desire to make a positive impact will be driven to overcome obstacles and keep moving forward.

Motivation also involves being resilient. Entrepreneurs often face setbacks and failures. Staying motivated in the face of these challenges requires a strong sense of purpose and determination. By maintaining a positive attitude and focusing on your goals, you can persevere through difficult times.

Additionally, motivation can inspire your team. Your passion and commitment can influence and motivate others. By sharing your vision and enthusiasm, you can create a sense of shared purpose and drive within your organization.

Moreover, motivation can enhance your creativity and innovation. When you are motivated, you are more likely to take risks and explore new ideas. This can lead to creative solutions and innovative products or services that set your business apart from the competition.

Tips for Boosting Motivation

Set clear goals

Define your long-term goals and break them down into achievable steps. This can help you stay focused and motivated.

Celebrate achievements

Recognize and celebrate your successes, no matter how small. This can boost morale and motivation.

Stay positive

Maintain a positive outlook and focus on your strengths. Positive thinking can keep you motivated even in challenging times.

Create a vision board

Visualize your goals and keep them in front of you as a constant reminder of what you are working towards.

Surround yourself with positive influences

Spend time with people who inspire and support you.

Take breaks

Give yourself time to rest and recharge to avoid burnout.

By developing motivation, you can stay focused on your goals and inspire others to achieve great things. This skill is essential for driving success and innovation in entrepreneurship.

How These Dimensions Work Together

These dimensions of Emotional Intelligence don't work in isolation. They interact and support each other. For example, self-awareness can help you understand your emotions, which aids in self-regulation. Empathy can improve your social skills, and motivation can drive you to develop all these areas further.

Understanding how these dimensions work together is crucial for developing strong EI. For instance, an empathetic leader who is also self-aware and can regulate their emotions will be better equipped to handle team conflicts and inspire their team. Combining these skills creates a well-rounded approach to leadership and decision-making.

By developing a balanced set of EI skills, entrepreneurs can create a robust foundation for their business. This involves not only honing each skill individually but also understanding how they complement and reinforce each other.

Tips for Developing Emotional Intelligence

Self-Awareness

Keep a journal and practice mindfulness.

Self-Regulation

Pause before reacting and develop healthy coping strategies.

Empathy

Listen actively and ask open-ended questions.

Social Skills

Communicate clearly and build rapport.

Motivation

Set clear goals and celebrate achievements.

These tips provide practical steps for developing each dimension of EI. By incorporating these practices into your daily routine, you can enhance your emotional intelligence and improve your effectiveness as an entrepreneur.

REAL-WORLD EXAMPLES

Consider Howard Schultz, the former CEO of Starbucks. His empathy and social skills helped him create a positive company culture. He understood the importance of treating employees well, which in turn led to better customer service and business success.

Another example is Richard Branson, founder of Virgin Group. His motivation and ability to connect with people have been key to his success. Branson's social skills and empathy have helped him build strong relationships with his employees and partners, driving his companies to great heights.

Real-world examples like Howard Schultz and Richard Branson show how emotional intelligence works in practice. They provide inspiration and proof that developing EI can lead to significant achievements. Studying the experiences of successful entrepreneurs can offer valuable insights and motivation.

CONCLUSION

Emotional intelligence is a crucial skill for entrepreneurs. It involves understanding and managing your own emotions, as well as recognizing and influencing the emotions of others. By developing self-awareness, self-regulation, empathy, social skills, and motivation, you can enhance your leadership, decision-making, and relationships. In the next chapter, we will explore how these emotional intelligence skills can be applied to building and leading successful teams.

CHAPTER 3

HOW SUCCESSFUL ENTREPRENEURS MASTER RISK AND REWARD

Imagine standing at the edge of a cliff, knowing that success lies on the other side. Will you take the leap or stay on solid ground? You can stand right here where you are safe, or you can run as fast as you can, jumping as high and as far as you can. You might fall. Or you might make it to the other side.

This is the essence of entrepreneurship. Balancing on the edge, weighing the risks and rewards, and deciding to move forward despite the uncertainty. For entrepreneurs, risk is a constant companion. It's not just a part of the journey; it is the journey. Understanding and managing this risk can mean the difference between soaring success and staggering failure.

In this chapter, we will explore how entrepreneurs can navigate the uncertainties they face every day. We will look at different types of risks, how to assess and prioritize them, and how to develop a mindset that embraces risk as an opportunity for growth.

Let's start by understanding the entrepreneurial approach to risk.

Understanding the Entrepreneurial Approach to Risk

Entrepreneurs face risk every day. It's part of the job. But understanding and managing risk can make the difference between success and failure. This section will help you navigate these uncertainties with confidence.

Risk in entrepreneurship comes in many forms. It can be financial, operational, market-related, or personal. Financial risks involve losing money, like when an investment doesn't pay off. Operational risks come from internal processes, such as a critical system failing. Market risks are about competition and changes in the market, like a new competitor entering your space. Personal risks involve your time, money, and well-being, such as the stress of long working hours.

Entrepreneurs must embrace risk. Without it, there is no innovation or growth. Viewing risk as an integral part of business is essential. Successful entrepreneurs don't shy away from risk; they manage it. They weigh the potential downsides against the possible rewards and make informed decisions.

Assessing risk is a crucial skill. It's about identifying potential risks and evaluating their likelihood and impact. This isn't a one-time task. It's an ongoing process since risks can change over time. Regular assessment helps prioritize risks, focusing on those that pose the greatest threat or opportunity. Using tools like SWOT analysis (Strengths, Weaknesses, Opportunities, Threats) can provide a comprehensive view of internal and external factors that could impact your business.

Knowing your risk tolerance is also crucial. Everyone has different comfort levels with risk. Understanding your tolerance helps in making decisions that align with your goals. It prevents taking on too much risk or being overly cautious. Entrepreneurs with a high tolerance for risk might be more willing to invest in bold, innovative ideas, while those with lower tolerance may prefer safer, more predictable ventures.

Effective risk management requires strategies. This might include diversifying investments, creating contingency plans, or securing insurance. For example, diversifying your product line can spread financial risk. Contingency plans prepare you for potential setbacks, ensuring your business can continue operating during crises. Securing insurance can protect against specific risks, such as property damage or liability claims. Good risk management is about being prepared for the worst while aiming for the best.

Learning from both successes and failures is vital. Every risk taken offers lessons. Analyze what worked and what didn't. Use these insights for future decisions. For example, if a marketing campaign fails, examine why it didn't work. Did it reach the wrong audience? Was the message unclear? Understanding these factors can help improve future campaigns.

Understanding risk involves recognizing various types, assessing and prioritizing them, knowing your tolerance, and developing management strategies. It's about balancing potential rewards with possible losses. This approach can help move your business forward confidently.

Understanding and managing risk is fundamental for any entrepreneur. But knowing how to assess these risks is equally important. Accurate risk assessment allows you to make informed decisions and prioritize effectively.

Now let's delve into the tools and techniques for assessing risks, helping you identify and evaluate the challenges your business might face. This will equip you with the knowledge to navigate uncertainties and seize opportunities with confidence.

Tools and Techniques for Assessing Risk

Accurately assessing risks is essential for entrepreneurs. It helps make informed decisions and prioritize effectively.

To start, you need to identify potential risks. This includes considering market trends, competition, technological changes, regulations, finances, and operations. Identifying these risks is the first step in managing them effectively.

Using tools like SWOT analysis can be helpful. SWOT stands for Strengths, Weaknesses, Opportunities, and Threats. This tool provides a comprehensive view of the internal and external factors that could impact your business.

For example, strengths might include your team's expertise, while weaknesses could be limited resources. Opportunities might be new market trends, and threats could be emerging competitors. By mapping these out, you gain a clearer picture of where risks might arise.

Once risks are identified, analyze their impact and likelihood. Use both qualitative and quantitative approaches.

Qualitative analysis might include expert opinions and brainstorming.

Quantitative analysis could involve financial projections and statistical models.

For instance, you might estimate the financial loss if a key supplier fails or use historical data to predict market trends. The goal is to understand each risk's nature, severity, and probability.

Prioritize risks based on their impact and likelihood. Not all risks are equal. Some are minor, while others can threaten your business's survival.

Focus on the most critical risks first. This helps allocate resources effectively. For example, if a potential regulatory change could significantly impact your operations, prioritize developing a compliance strategy over less critical issues.

Regularly revisit and update your risk assessments.

The business environment changes constantly, and so do the risks. Regular reviews help stay ahead of potential threats and capitalize on emerging opportunities.

For example, new technological advances might introduce both risks and opportunities. Keeping your assessments current ensures you're prepared for these changes.

Understand your business's risk appetite.

This is the balance between potential rewards and your willingness to take risks

It's influenced by the business stage, financial stability, and personal tolerance for uncertainty. For instance, a startup might have a higher risk appetite compared to an established business.

Knowing this helps in making decisions that align with your goals and capacity to handle risk.

Seek input from different stakeholders.

Employees, partners, advisors, and even customers can provide valuable insights. This diverse perspective leads to a more comprehensive risk assessment.

For example, employees might identify operational risks you hadn't considered, while customers might highlight market risks related to changing preferences.

Engaging various stakeholders ensures a well-rounded view of potential risks.

Leverage technology for risk assessment.

Tools like data analytics, AI, and predictive modeling offer deep insights. They can help you understand market trends, customer behaviors, and operational efficiencies.

For example, AI can analyze large datasets to identify patterns and predict future risks, such as supply chain disruptions. Leveraging these technologies enhances accuracy and efficiency, helping you make more informed decisions.

Assessing risks involves identifying, analyzing, prioritizing, and monitoring them. It requires qualitative and quantitative methods, continuous evaluation, and diverse perspectives.

Using technology enhances accuracy and efficiency, helping you navigate uncertainties confidently.

Having a clear process for assessing risks is crucial, but it's only part of the equation. Building a mindset that embraces risk is equally important. This mindset helps you view risk as an opportunity rather than a threat.

Next we'll explore how to develop a risk-tolerant mindset, allowing you to face uncertainties with confidence and turn potential challenges into growth opportunities.

BUILDING A RICK-TOLERANT MINDSET

Developing a risk-tolerant mindset is crucial for entrepreneurs. It's about embracing uncertainty and using it to your advantage. This mindset doesn't mean being reckless. It means recognizing that risk can lead to opportunity and growth.

Start by changing how you view risk. See it as a positive force. Without risk, there are no new ideas or innovations. Entrepreneurs with this mindset view risks as challenges to overcome.

Embrace uncertainty.

The path of entrepreneurship is never clear or straightforward. Accepting that uncertainty is part of the journey.

Let go of the need for complete control and be open to new experiences. Consider keeping a journal (have I said this before?) to reflect on how you handle uncertainty, noting any patterns or insights that emerge.

Learn from failure.

Entrepreneurs who are comfortable with risk understand that failure is a learning experience.

Analyze your failures. Extract lessons and apply this knowledge to future endeavors. This transforms setbacks into steps toward success.

Conduct a post-mortem analysis on failed projects, asking questions like, "What went wrong?" and "What can we do differently next time?" to gain valuable insights.

Build resilience.

This allows you to bounce back from setbacks.

Maintain a positive attitude and see challenges as temporary hurdles.

Stay focused on your vision.

Engage in activities that build mental and emotional resilience, such as mindfulness, exercise, and connecting with supportive friends or mentors.

Resilient entrepreneurs don't let setbacks derail their progress but use them as opportunities to grow stronger.

Take calculated risks.

Evaluate the potential rewards against the possible downsides. Use data, insights, and intuition to make informed decisions.

Know when to take a leap of faith and when to hold back.

Develop a decision-making framework that includes risk assessment tools like SWOT analysis and scenario planning.

This structured approach helps ensure that risks are well understood and managed.

Balance optimism with realism.

Have a positive outlook and believe in your vision. But stay grounded. This balance helps make hopeful yet pragmatic decisions.

Set realistic goals and timelines and adjust them as needed based on new information. This way, you can remain optimistic about your vision while adjusting to stay on track.

Keep learning and adapting.

The business world is always changing. What worked yesterday might not work today.

Be a lifelong learner. Update your knowledge and skills to stay ahead. This helps you adapt strategies and take risks aligned with market dynamics.

Take courses, attend workshops, and read industry publications to stay informed about the latest trends and best practices.

Leverage a support network.

Mentors, advisors, and peers provide valuable insights and perspectives. They can guide, encourage, and offer a sounding board for decisions.

Join entrepreneurial networks or mastermind groups where you can share experiences and gain advice from others who have faced similar challenges.

This network can be invaluable for navigating tough decisions and staying motivated.

Practice decision-making under pressure.

Entrepreneurs often need to make decisions quickly and under pressure. Practicing this skill can help you become more comfortable with it.

Simulate high-pressure scenarios and make decisions within a set timeframe. This practice helps build confidence and improves your ability to make sound decisions in real-life situations.

Set small, manageable goals.

Breaking down big risks into smaller, more manageable tasks can make them less daunting. Set short-term goals that lead to your larger objectives.

This approach helps maintain momentum and reduces the fear associated with taking big risks.

Celebrate small wins.

Acknowledge and celebrate your achievements, no matter how small. This boosts morale and reinforces a positive attitude towards risk-taking.

Recognizing progress keeps you motivated and helps you stay focused on your long-term vision.

Building a risk-tolerant mindset involves changing how you view risk, embracing uncertainty, learning from failure, building resilience, taking calculated risks, balancing optimism with realism, continuous learning, leveraging a support network, practicing decision-making under pressure, setting small goals, and celebrating wins.

This mindset helps seize opportunities and navigate challenges confidently.

Risk is inherent in entrepreneurship, but managing it effectively is key to success.

Mitigating risk involves taking bold steps while being prepared for potential pitfalls. Effective risk mitigation isn't about eliminating risks but managing them to maximize opportunities and minimize downsides.

Let’s explore practical strategies for balancing boldness with caution, ensuring your business is prepared to handle uncertainties while pursuing growth.

Balancing Boldness and Caution with Risk Mitigation

Mitigating risk is about balancing boldness with caution. It's essential in the unpredictable world of business.

Effective risk mitigation isn't about eliminating risks but managing them to maximize opportunities and minimize downsides.

Identify potential risks first.

The first step is to figure out what risks your business might face.

Risks come in many forms.

There are financial risks, or things that could cause you to lose money. This might include slow sales, increased costs, or bad investments.

Operational risks are anything that would disrupt the day-to-day operation of the business. This could be equipment failures, supply chain issues, or employee mistakes.

Market risks are outside market forces that affect you. Think about new competitors, changing customer preferences, or economic downturns.

Regulatory Risks are laws that could impact your business. This might include new taxes or changes to industry rules.

Let's say you run a small bakery. Some risks you might face are increasing costs of ingredients, a supplier failing to deliver flour, gluten-free diets trending, or new taxes on sugary foods.

Evaluate risks based on their likelihood and impact.

Not all risks are equal. Some are minor, while others can threaten your business's survival.

Focus on the most critical risks first.

This helps allocate resources effectively.

If you were to rank the risks we've identified for our bakery by likelihood and impact they'd be:

1. A supplier failing to deliver flour
2. Increased costs of ingredients
3. Trending diets like gluten-free
4. New taxes on sugary foods
5. Develop a risk mitigation plan.

This plan should outline strategies to avoid, reduce, transfer, or accept risks.

Avoidance might involve changing plans to bypass high-risk activities.

Reduction could include safety measures or quality controls.

Transferring risk might involve purchasing insurance.

Acceptance means recognizing some risks are inherent and preparing to manage them.

For instance, having multiple suppliers can minimize financial risk, stocking extra flour and get you passed a failed delivery, and offering sugar-free and gluten-free options can help you avoid losing business to fad diets.

Diversify your operations.

Don't rely on a single product, market, or revenue stream.

Diversification spreads risk and ensures that one failure doesn't ruin your business.

For example, if cupcakes face a market downturn, offering sandwiches and coffee can keep your business stable.

This approach also applies to suppliers and partnerships to avoid dependency on a single source.

Prepare contingency plans.

Plan for worst-case scenarios.

Have backup suppliers, financial reserves, and alternative strategies. Contingency plans provide a safety net.

For example, if a key supplier fails to deliver flour, having a list of alternate suppliers ensures that your operations continue smoothly.

Financial reserves can help you weather economic downturns without making drastic cuts.

Regularly monitor and review risks and mitigation strategies.

The business environment changes constantly, and so do the risks.

Regular reviews help stay ahead of potential threats and capitalize on emerging opportunities.

For example, new technological advances might introduce both risks and opportunities.

Keeping your assessments current ensures you're prepared for these changes.

Foster a risk-aware culture.

Train employees to recognize and respond to risks. Communicate risk management policies clearly.

Encourage open discussions about risks. Empower employees to take proactive steps in managing risks.

This culture ensures that risk management is everyone's responsibility, not just top management. For instance, frontline employees might spot operational risks that higher-ups could miss.

Manage finances wisely.

Ensure your business is financially robust. Maintain healthy cash flow, manage debts, and have a clear financial strategy.

Financial stability provides a buffer against uncertainties. For example, keeping a portion of your revenue as a reserve can help you navigate through unexpected financial challenges.

Leverage technology for risk mitigation.

Previously mentioned AI tools can also be useful for risk mitigation.

Data analytics and predictive modeling offer deep insights into potential risks. They help you understand market trends, customer behaviors, and operational efficiencies.

AI can analyze large datasets to identify patterns and predict future risks like supply chain disruptions. Leveraging these technologies enhances accuracy and efficiency, helping you make more informed decisions.

Risk mitigation involves identifying, evaluating, and prioritizing risks, developing a mitigation plan, diversifying operations, preparing contingency plans, regular monitoring, fostering a risk-aware culture, managing finances wisely, and leveraging technology.

This balanced approach enables you to pursue your vision confidently.

Understanding how to mitigate risks is crucial, but learning from failures is just as important. Failures offer valuable lessons that can drive future success. Embracing failure as a learning opportunity can transform setbacks into steppingstones. Let's delve into how to turn failures into opportunities and build a resilient entrepreneurial mindset.

Turn Setbacks into Opportunities by Learning from Failure

In the journey of entrepreneurship, setbacks are inevitable.

However, they are also invaluable learning opportunities.

Embracing failure can transform setbacks into valuable lessons for future success.

Here's how to effectively learn from failure and build a resilient entrepreneurial mindset.

Accept failure as part of the process.

The first step is to accept that failure is a natural part of the entrepreneurial journey.

Not every idea will succeed, and not every venture will flourish. Entrepreneurs who understand this are better equipped to handle setbacks. They see failure not as a reflection of their worth but as an opportunity to learn and grow.

Analyze failures objectively.

Once a setback occurs, take a step back and analyze what happened.

Objectivity is crucial here.

Avoid blaming yourself or others. Instead, focus on understanding the root causes of the failure.

Conduct a post-mortem analysis and ask questions like:

What went wrong?

Were there any warning signs that were missed?

Were the assumptions or strategies flawed?

Did external factors play a significant role?

By answering these questions, you can identify patterns and insights that will be valuable for future endeavors.

Embrace a growth mindset.

A growth mindset is the belief that abilities and intelligence can be developed through dedication and hard work.

Entrepreneurs with this mindset view setbacks as opportunities to improve their skills and knowledge. They understand that failure is not a dead end but a detour that provides valuable lessons.

This mindset encourages resilience and continuous learning.

Communicate openly about setbacks.

Discussing failures openly with your team, mentors, or peers can provide new perspectives and support. Sharing your experiences helps maintain transparency and trust within your organization.

It also fosters a culture where failure is seen as a learning opportunity rather than a source of shame.

This open communication can lead to valuable feedback and collective problem-solving.

Maintain perspective.

In the face of a setback, it's easy to lose sight of the bigger picture. Maintaining perspective is essential. Remember past successes and acknowledge the progress you've made.

Focus on your long-term goals and understand that setbacks are just temporary obstacles. This broader view helps you stay motivated and resilient.

Build emotional resilience.

Setbacks can be emotionally draining. Developing emotional resilience is key to bouncing back. Manage stress through practices like mindfulness, exercise, and hobbies. Seek support from friends, family, or professional counselors if needed. Building emotional resilience helps you stay balanced and focused during tough times.

Be adaptable.

Sometimes, a setback requires significant changes in your strategy or direction.

Be willing to pivot and adapt based on the insights gained from failures.

Flexibility is crucial in entrepreneurship.

Use what you've learned to make informed adjustments and explore new opportunities.

Recommit to your vision.

After a setback, reaffirm your commitment to your vision and goals.

Remind yourself why you started your entrepreneurial journey in the first place. Align your actions with your long-term objectives.

This recommitment provides a renewed sense of purpose and direction.

Create a culture that values learning.

Encourage a culture within your organization that values learning from failure. Promote risk-taking and experimentation.

When employees know that failure is seen as a learning opportunity, they are more likely to innovate and take initiative.

This culture fosters creativity and resilience.

Learning from failure involves accepting it as a natural part of the process, analyzing setbacks objectively, embracing a growth mindset, communicating openly, maintaining perspective, building emotional resilience, being adaptable, recommitting to your vision, and creating a culture that values learning. These practices turn setbacks into valuable learning experiences, helping you build a resilient entrepreneurial mindset and drive your business toward success.

Understanding how to learn from failure and turn setbacks into opportunities is crucial for any entrepreneur. By accepting failure as part of the process, analyzing setbacks objectively, embracing a growth mindset, and fostering a culture that values learning, you can build resilience and continuously improve your strategies.

With these insights, you are better equipped to face the uncertainties of entrepreneurship. Now, let's bring together all these elements to fully embrace the entrepreneurship mindset, combining risk management and resilience with a clear, forward-thinking vision.

Conclusion

Navigating risk and reward in entrepreneurship requires understanding and managing various types of risks. It involves developing a risk-tolerant mindset, assessing, and prioritizing risks, mitigating them effectively, and learning from failures. By embracing these strategies, entrepreneurs can confidently navigate uncertainties, seize opportunities, and drive their ventures toward success.

In Chapter 3, we delved into understanding and managing risk, emphasizing how to learn from failures to build a resilient entrepreneurial mindset. These skills are crucial for handling uncertainties and turning setbacks into opportunities for growth.

Chapter 4, "Mastering Resilience," builds on these concepts by focusing on the psychological and emotional aspects of resilience. This chapter explores techniques and strategies to maintain mental toughness and perseverance. It discusses how to stay motivated, manage stress, and remain adaptable in the face of ongoing challenges. The resilience we develop from managing risks and learning from failures is the foundation for overcoming obstacles and achieving long-term success in our entrepreneurial journey.

By connecting the principles of risk management and the lessons learned from failure, we prepare ourselves to cultivate a resilient mindset. This resilience is essential not just for surviving the entrepreneurial journey but for thriving within it.

CHAPTER 4

WHAT SUCCESSFUL ENTREPRENEURS KNOW ABOUT GRIT AND RESILIENCE

Think about Rocky Balboa standing up after every knockdown. What if you could learn how to channel that same resilience, turning every setback into a setup for your next victory?

This chapter will teach you how to build the resilience needed to overcome any challenge and keep moving forward.

Rocky Balboa didn't win because he avoided getting hit; he won because he got back up every time. Is it possible to develop that kind of resilience in your entrepreneurial journey?

I will show you how to cultivate resilience, ensuring you stay strong no matter what life throws at you. By the end of this chapter, you'll feel more empowered, think more strategically about setbacks, and approach your entrepreneurial journey with newfound strength and confidence.

Resilience is what keeps Rocky Balboa getting back up, and it's what will keep you moving forward in your entrepreneurial journey. But what exactly is resilience? How do you build it, and why is it so vital for your success? Let's dive into the essence of resilience in entrepreneurship, exploring the mindset and practices that will help you bounce back stronger from every challenge you face.

THE ESSENCE OF RESILIENCE IN ENTREPRENEURSHIP

Resilience is about bouncing back from tough times and not giving up when things get hard. For entrepreneurs, it means using challenges to grow and get better.

Resilience starts with the right mindset.

Entrepreneurs with a resilient mindset see problems as chances to learn and improve rather than as dead ends.

A resilient mindset involves viewing obstacles as puzzles to solve.

This perspective is crucial because the path of entrepreneurship is rarely smooth or straightforward. It's filled with unexpected challenges and setbacks.

Having a resilient mindset allows entrepreneurs to navigate these challenges effectively.

Adaptability is key to resilience. The business world changes fast, and entrepreneurs who can adapt to these changes are more likely to survive and thrive.

Emotional strength is also important in resilience. Running a business can be incredibly stressful. Resilient entrepreneurs handle stress without falling apart. They maintain a positive outlook even when things are tough and don't let negative emotions derail their progress. Managing these emotions is crucial, as they can otherwise cloud judgment and lead to poor decisions.

Perseverance means sticking with your goals, even when it's hard. Resilient entrepreneurs keep going. They don’t quit at the first sign of trouble. They understand that success often requires long-term effort and commitment. This perseverance is what often separates successful entrepreneurs from those who don’t make it.

Self-care is crucial for building resilience. Entrepreneurs need to take care of their health to maintain their energy and focus. This includes eating well, exercising regularly, and getting enough sleep. Neglecting self-care can lead to burnout, which can undermine resilience and overall effectiveness.

Support systems are equally important. Having friends, family, and mentors can provide emotional support and practical advice. These relationships offer encouragement and help entrepreneurs stay grounded during tough times. A strong support network can make the difference between giving up and finding the strength to keep going.

A learning mindset also helps build resilience. Entrepreneurs should always look for ways to improve and learn from both successes and failures. This mindset involves being open to feedback and willing to make changes based on new information. It's about seeing every experience as an opportunity to grow.

Finding meaning in your work is another component of resilience. This deeper purpose provides motivation and a reason to keep going, even when faced with significant challenges. For many entrepreneurs, this sense of purpose is about more than just making money. It's about making a difference or achieving a personal vision.

Entrepreneurs can also build resilient teams. A positive work culture that encourages open communication and supports employee well-being can significantly enhance team resilience. When employees feel valued and supported, they are more likely to stay engaged and motivated, even in difficult times.

Resilience is about having the right mindset, being adaptable, and managing emotions effectively. It's about persevering through challenges, taking care of yourself, and learning from experiences. It's about finding purpose in your work and building strong, supportive teams.

By cultivating these qualities, entrepreneurs can better navigate the ups and downs of their journey and emerge stronger from each challenge.

Developing Grit, The Power of Passion and Perseverance

Grit is the drive that keeps entrepreneurs going, combining passion and perseverance. Passion is a deep love for your work, motivating you to push forward even when things get tough. It's what gets you up in the morning and keeps you working late into the night. Passionate entrepreneurs are driven by a love for their work and a desire to make a difference.

Perseverance means sticking with your goals over the long term. Entrepreneurs with grit don't give up easily. They know that success takes time and effort, and they are prepared to work hard to achieve their vision. Perseverance involves being consistent in your efforts, even when progress is slow, or obstacles arise.

A growth mindset is crucial for developing grit. This means believing that abilities and intelligence can be developed with practice and effort. Entrepreneurs with a growth mindset see challenges as opportunities to learn and grow. They are not deterred by failures; instead, they view them as a natural part of the learning process.

Clear goals help maintain focus and direction. Setting specific, measurable, achievable, relevant, and time-bound (SMART) goals can guide your efforts and keep you on track. Break big goals into smaller, manageable steps. This makes them less overwhelming and easier to achieve, providing a sense of progress and accomplishment along the way.

Discipline is key to perseverance. Entrepreneurs need to stay on track and avoid distractions. This means establishing and maintaining routines that support your goals. Disciplined entrepreneurs are methodical in their approach, ensuring that every action aligns with their broader objectives. This consistency is crucial for long-term success.

Building mental and emotional strength is also important. This helps you stay balanced and focused, even when faced with challenges. Practices like mindfulness, meditation, and regular exercise can help build this strength. These activities promote mental clarity, reduce stress, and enhance emotional resilience.

Seeking inspiration from others can also build grit. Learning from mentors and role models can provide valuable insights and motivation. Their stories of overcoming challenges and achieving success can inspire you to keep going, even when things are tough. Surrounding yourself with positive influences can reinforce your own determination and drive.

Developing grit involves cultivating both passion and perseverance. It means having a growth mindset and setting clear, achievable goals. It requires discipline and emotional strength to stay focused and consistent. And it's about finding inspiration from others who have faced similar challenges. By building these qualities, entrepreneurs can develop the grit needed to pursue their vision with relentless determination.

Coping Strategies for Entrepreneurial Stress

Entrepreneurship can be stressful. Managing stress effectively is crucial for maintaining personal well-being and business success. Coping strategies are not about eliminating stress entirely but about managing it so that it doesn't become overwhelming or debilitating.

Time management is key to coping with stress. Entrepreneurs often face many demands on their time, which can lead to feeling overwhelmed. Effective time management involves prioritizing tasks, setting realistic goals, and delegating responsibilities when necessary. Tools like time-blocking, to-do lists, and digital organizers can help manage time more efficiently.

A strong support network is important for managing stress. This can include family, friends, mentors, and peers. Having people to talk to and share experiences with can provide emotional relief and practical solutions to stress-inducing challenges. Networking groups, online forums, and professional associations can also be valuable sources of support and guidance.

Mindfulness and relaxation techniques are effective for reducing stress. Practices like meditation, deep breathing exercises, and yoga can help calm the mind and reduce anxiety. These techniques provide a way to disconnect from the pressures of work, even if only for a short period, allowing for mental and emotional rejuvenation.

Physical health is closely tied to stress management. Regular exercise, a healthy diet, and adequate sleep are essential for maintaining physical and mental resilience. Exercise is a powerful stress reliever that releases endorphins, improves mood, and enhances overall well-being. Maintaining a healthy lifestyle helps entrepreneurs cope with stress more effectively and maintain the energy needed to manage their businesses.

Setting boundaries between work and personal life is crucial for preventing burnout. This involves defining clear limits for work hours and personal time, ensuring that work doesn't spill over into personal life. Setting boundaries might involve specific work hours, dedicated time for family and hobbies, and learning to say no to non-essential commitments. This balance is essential for maintaining overall well-being.

A positive mindset helps manage stress. Maintaining a positive outlook, focusing on solutions rather than problems, and practicing gratitude can significantly impact how stress is perceived and managed. A positive mindset fosters resilience and helps entrepreneurs view challenges as opportunities for growth and learning.

Sometimes, professional help is needed to manage stress effectively. This can include consulting with a therapist, counselor, or coach. Professional guidance can provide new perspectives, coping strategies, and tools for managing stress, anxiety, and other mental health issues. Seeking help when needed is a sign of strength, not weakness.

Managing stress involves effective time management and a strong support network. Mindfulness and physical health are important components, as are setting boundaries and maintaining a positive mindset. Sometimes, seeking professional help is necessary. By implementing these strategies, entrepreneurs can manage stress effectively, maintain their health and well-being, and navigate the demands and challenges of running a business.

LEARNING FROM SETBACKS

Setbacks are a natural part of entrepreneurship. Learning from them is crucial for growth and improvement. It involves adopting a mindset that sees setbacks as opportunities to learn and refine strategies.

Reflecting on setbacks helps understand what went wrong. Take time to analyze the situation, identify mistakes, and consider what could have been done differently. Ask tough questions: Were there warning signs? Were assumptions flawed? This reflection helps prevent similar mistakes in the future.

A growth mindset is key to learning from setbacks. Entrepreneurs with a growth mindset believe that abilities and intelligence can be developed through effort and learning. They view setbacks as part of the journey, not the end. This mindset encourages resilience by shifting the focus from proving oneself to improving oneself.

Effective communication is crucial when dealing with setbacks. Discuss setbacks openly with your team, stakeholders, or mentors. Sharing experiences can provide new insights, support, and different perspectives. It also helps maintain transparency and trust within the team.

Maintaining perspective is important. In the face of a setback, it's easy to lose sight of the bigger picture and get bogged down by negativity. Keeping perspective involves remembering past successes, acknowledging progress made, and focusing on long-term goals. This broader perspective helps keep setbacks in context and maintain motivation.

Building emotional resilience helps manage the emotional impact of setbacks. Setbacks can be emotionally taxing, leading to feelings of disappointment, frustration, or doubt. Developing emotional resilience involves managing these emotions effectively, seeking support when needed, and finding ways to stay positive and motivated. Practices like mindfulness, exercise, and hobbies can help manage emotional responses.

Adaptability is crucial when dealing with setbacks. Sometimes a setback might require a significant pivot in strategy, a change in product direction, or a reevaluation of the target market. Adaptable entrepreneurs are willing to make these changes. They remain flexible and open to new directions, using the insights gained from setbacks to guide their next steps.

Recommitting to your vision and goals is important after a setback. This gives you a renewed sense of purpose and direction. It involves reaffirming why you started the entrepreneurial journey and aligning your actions with your long-term objectives. This recommitment provides motivation to keep moving forward.

Learning from setbacks involves reflection and a growth mindset. Effective communication and maintaining perspective are key. Building emotional resilience and adaptability helps manage the impact of setbacks. Recommitting to your vision keeps you focused and motivated. By adopting these practices, entrepreneurs can turn setbacks into valuable learning experiences and build a resilient mindset.

LONG-TERM STRATEGIES FOR SUSTAINING RESILIENCE

Sustaining resilience over the long term is essential for entrepreneurial success. It involves building practices that help you stay strong and handle ongoing challenges effectively. This ensures you can navigate the rough waters of business with strength and agility.

A resilient mindset is the foundation for long-term resilience. This mindset is characterized by a positive attitude, a willingness to learn and adapt, and an unwavering commitment to one's vision. Cultivating such a mindset involves regular self-reflection, affirming one’s strengths and achievements, and maintaining a clear focus on long-term goals. It also means embracing challenges as opportunities for growth and seeing change as an inevitable part of the entrepreneurial journey.

Consistent self-care is crucial for long-term resilience. This includes regular exercise, a balanced diet, adequate sleep, and mindfulness practices. Self-care also means taking time off to recharge, pursuing hobbies and interests outside of work, and maintaining healthy relationships. Entrepreneurs who prioritize their well-being can better handle stress, maintain high energy levels, and keep a clear focus on their goals.

Building and leveraging a support network is important for sustaining resilience. No entrepreneur can do it alone. A robust support network—comprising family, friends, mentors, advisors, and peers—provides emotional support, practical advice, and diverse perspectives. This network can be a source of strength in challenging times and a sounding board for new ideas and strategies. Actively building and nurturing these relationships is crucial for long-term resilience.

Continuous learning and adaptation are essential for sustaining resilience. The business world is dynamic, and what works today may not work tomorrow. Sustaining resilience requires a commitment to continuous learning and adaptation. This involves staying abreast of industry trends, acquiring new skills, and being open to new business models and strategies. Entrepreneurs who are lifelong learners are better equipped to adapt to changes and seize new opportunities.

Practicing gratitude and positive thinking is important for maintaining a positive outlook. Focus on the positive aspects of your journey and celebrate successes, no matter how small. Practicing gratitude can significantly impact your mental and emotional well-being. It helps maintain a balanced perspective and fosters a sense of contentment and motivation.

Setting realistic expectations and boundaries is crucial for preventing burnout. Unrealistic expectations and a lack of boundaries can lead to burnout and decreased resilience. Entrepreneurs need to set achievable goals, recognize their limits, and learn to say no to demands that exceed their capacity. Setting clear boundaries between work and personal life is also crucial for maintaining long-term resilience.

Embracing flexibility and openness to change is key to sustaining resilience. This means being willing to pivot strategies, explore new markets, and revise goals as needed. A flexible approach allows entrepreneurs to respond effectively to unexpected challenges and opportunities, keeping their businesses agile and resilient.

Financial prudence and planning are important for sustaining resilience. Financial challenges are a major source of stress for entrepreneurs. Long-term resilience requires prudent financial management, including maintaining a healthy cash flow, setting aside reserves for tough times, and planning for future investments. Financial stability provides a buffer against uncertainties and enables entrepreneurs to make decisions from a position of strength.

Sustaining resilience involves cultivating a resilient mindset, consistent self-care, and building a strong support network. Continuous learning, practicing gratitude, and setting realistic expectations are key. Embracing flexibility and maintaining financial stability helps keep you adaptable and prepared for challenges. By adopting these strategies, entrepreneurs can maintain their strength, agility, and focus over the long term, turning the challenges of entrepreneurship into opportunities for growth and success.

CONCLUSION

Resilience and grit are crucial for entrepreneurs. They help you bounce back from setbacks and keep going. Developing these traits involves mindset, self-care, and support systems. It's about learning from experiences and staying adaptable. Long-term resilience requires continuous learning and a positive outlook. With these strategies, entrepreneurs can thrive in the face of challenges.

Now that you understand how to build resilience and grit to navigate setbacks, it's time to unlock your creative potential. In the next chapter, we will explore how to cultivate innovative thinking and turn creative ideas into actionable strategies. Just as resilience helps you stay the course, creativity will fuel your growth and keep your entrepreneurial journey dynamic and exciting. Get ready to learn how to unleash your creativity and drive innovation in your business.

CHAPTER 5

HOW SUCCESSFUL ENTREPRENEURS HARNESS CREATIVE THINKING

Creativity is key to success in entrepreneurship. It drives innovation and helps solve problems. This chapter will show you how to unlock your creative potential and turn ideas into reality. By the end, you will have practical strategies to enhance creativity and foster innovation in your business.

FOSTERING AN IDEATION-FRIENDLY ENVIRONMENT

Creating an environment that encourages idea generation is crucial. Start by designing workspaces that stimulate creativity. Include areas for collaboration, relaxation, and solo work. Make the space welcoming and comfortable.

Encourage a culture where new ideas are valued. Promote open communication and ensure everyone feels heard. Create an atmosphere where experimentation is encouraged, and failure is seen as a learning opportunity. This psychological safety boosts creativity.

Regular brainstorming sessions can help generate ideas. Use different techniques like mind mapping and free writing. Make sure these sessions are judgment-free. The goal is to produce as many ideas as possible.

Provide the necessary tools and resources. Have whiteboards, sticky notes, and markers available. Digital tools like brainstorming software can also be helpful. Ensure the environment is conducive to creative thinking.

Consider the physical layout of your workspace. Natural light, comfortable seating, and inspiring decor can influence creativity. Quiet areas for focused work and open spaces for group discussions can balance different needs.

Encourage breaks and downtime. Creativity often flourishes when people have time to relax and recharge. Provide spaces for casual interactions and leisure activities. This can lead to spontaneous idea generation.

Implementing Regular Brainstorming Sessions

Brainstorming is a powerful tool for idea generation. Hold regular sessions to keep the creative juices flowing. Encourage participation from all team members. Different perspectives lead to better ideas.

Use various brainstorming methods. Mind mapping can help visualize ideas and connections. Reverse thinking, where you think about how to create problems instead of solving them, can spark innovative solutions. Role-playing can help see issues from different viewpoints.

Keep the sessions focused but flexible. Start with a clear goal but allow ideas to flow freely. Encourage wild and unconventional ideas. Sometimes the best solutions come from the most unexpected places.

Set clear rules for brainstorming sessions. Ensure that everyone understands the goal and process. Encourage equal participation and discourage criticism. Focus on quantity over quality during the initial phase.

Follow up on brainstorming sessions. Review and refine the ideas generated. Prioritize the most promising ones and develop action plans. This ensures that brainstorming leads to tangible results.

Document the ideas generated during sessions. Use digital tools to capture and organize ideas. Share the outcomes with the team to keep everyone informed and engaged.

ENCOURAGING CROSS-DISCIPLINARY COLLABORATION

Innovation often happens when different fields intersect. Encourage collaboration between team members from various backgrounds. This diversity brings a richness of ideas and perspectives.

Create mixed teams for projects. Combine people with different skills and experiences. This can lead to unique solutions that might not emerge from a homogeneous group.

Facilitate cross-departmental meetings and discussions. Regularly mix up teams to work on different projects. This cross-pollination of ideas can lead to innovative breakthroughs.

Promote a culture of openness and curiosity. Encourage team members to learn about other departments and disciplines. Provide opportunities for cross-training and job rotation. This broadens their perspectives and enhances creativity.

Organize team-building activities that foster collaboration. Activities like workshops, hackathons, and off-site retreats can build strong relationships and encourage creative thinking. These interactions help break down silos and promote a collaborative culture.

Leverage technology to facilitate collaboration. Use collaboration tools and platforms to connect team members across different locations. Virtual brainstorming sessions and online forums can keep the ideas flowing, even in remote or hybrid work environments.

Practicing Observational Skills

Keen observation is a powerful source of creativity. Train yourself and your team to notice details others might miss. This can lead to new insights and ideas.

Pay attention to your surroundings. Notice patterns, trends, and anomalies. Draw inspiration from everyday experiences. Sometimes, the simplest observation can spark a great idea.

Encourage your team to be curious. Ask questions and explore different perspectives. This curiosity drives innovation and leads to better problem-solving.

Develop routines for regular observation. Set aside time each day to observe and reflect. Keep a journal to record your observations and ideas. This practice can help you recognize connections and opportunities.

Encourage active listening. During meetings and discussions, focus on understanding others' viewpoints. This can reveal new insights and inspire creative solutions.

Attend industry events, conferences, and trade shows. These gatherings provide opportunities to observe trends and innovations. They can also spark new ideas and connections.

LEVERAGING CREATIVE THINKING TOOLS AND TECHNIQUES

Many tools and techniques can enhance creative thinking. SCAMPER (Substitute, Combine, Adapt, Modify, Put to another use, Eliminate, Reverse) is one such method. It helps you think about existing products or processes in new ways.

The Six Thinking Hats technique can also be useful. This method involves looking at a problem from six different perspectives. Each "hat" represents a different type of thinking, such as logical, emotional, or creative.

The Five Whys technique involves asking "why" five times to get to the root of a problem. This can uncover new solutions and ideas. Regularly using these tools can structure your thinking and boost creativity.

Experiment with other creative thinking techniques like brainstorming, mind mapping, and lateral thinking. These methods can help you explore different angles and generate innovative solutions.

Combine multiple techniques for a comprehensive approach. For example, use SCAMPER to modify an idea and then apply mind mapping to explore its potential. This multi-faceted approach can enhance your creative process.

Encourage team members to learn and apply these techniques. Provide training and resources to help them master different methods. Create a toolkit of creative thinking techniques for easy reference.

Evaluate the effectiveness of different techniques. Track the outcomes of ideas generated through each method. This can help you identify the most productive techniques for your team.

Encouraging Individual Creativity Practices

Creativity is both a personal and a collaborative effort. Encourage team members to engage in individual creative practices. This can help them tap into their unique creative potential.

Activities like journaling, sketching, or solo brainstorming can be beneficial. They provide a space for personal reflection and idea generation. Encourage your team to set aside time for these practices regularly.

These individual activities can complement collaborative efforts. They allow for personal growth and innovation. When team members bring their individual ideas to the group, it enriches the overall creative process.

Provide resources and support for individual creativity. Offer access to creative tools, workshops, and materials. Encourage team members to pursue hobbies and interests outside of work.

Recognize and celebrate individual creative achievements. Highlight the contributions of team members who bring unique ideas. This recognition can motivate others to engage in individual creative practices.

Create opportunities for personal development. Encourage team members to attend conferences, take courses, and read widely. This continuous learning fuels individual creativity and innovation.

PROMOTING CONTINUOUS LEARNING AND CURIOSITY

A culture of continuous learning is fertile ground for creativity. Encourage your team to keep learning and exploring new ideas. Provide opportunities for professional development and exposure to new technologies.

Promote curiosity by encouraging team members to ask questions and seek out new experiences. This can lead to new insights and innovative solutions. A curious mindset is always looking for better ways to do things.

Provide resources like books, courses, and workshops. Encourage your team to share what they learn with each other. This collective learning fosters a creative and innovative environment.

Host regular learning sessions and workshops. Invite experts to share their knowledge and insights. These sessions can introduce new concepts and spark creative thinking.

Encourage a growth mindset. Help your team see challenges as opportunities to learn and grow. This mindset fosters resilience and a willingness to experiment.

Create a library of learning resources. Include books, articles, videos, and online courses. Make these resources easily accessible to your team.

Celebrate learning achievements. Recognize team members who pursue new knowledge and skills. This recognition reinforces the value of continuous learning.

Embracing Diverse Perspectives and Experiences

Diversity is a key driver of creativity. Encourage the sharing of different perspectives within your team. This includes diversity of thought, experience, and expertise.

Create an inclusive environment where everyone feels valued. Encourage open discussions and respect different viewpoints. This can lead to richer and more innovative ideas.

Diversity should extend to hiring practices. Aim to build a team with varied backgrounds and skills. This diversity will bring new ideas and approaches to your business.

Encourage team members to share their unique experiences. Host storytelling sessions where they can talk about their backgrounds and insights. This sharing can foster mutual understanding and spark new ideas.

Promote cross-cultural understanding. Organize cultural exchange activities and celebrate diverse holidays. These activities can enhance creativity by exposing the team to different traditions and ways of thinking.

Foster an environment of psychological safety. Ensure that all team members feel comfortable sharing their ideas without fear of judgment. This safety encourages openness and innovation.

Implementing Idea Management Systems

An idea management system can help capture and develop creative ideas. This ensures that valuable ideas are not lost and are given the attention they deserve.

Use tools like idea boards or digital platforms to collect ideas. Encourage team members to contribute regularly. Review and evaluate these ideas periodically.

Create a process for developing and implementing the best ideas. This shows your team that their contributions are valued and can lead to real changes. It also keeps the flow of innovation steady.

Document the ideas generated during sessions. Use digital tools to capture and organize ideas. Share the outcomes with the team to keep everyone informed and engaged.

Establish criteria for evaluating ideas. Consider factors like feasibility, impact, and alignment with business goals. This evaluation ensures that the best ideas move forward.

Provide feedback on submitted ideas. Let team members know the status of their ideas and any next steps. This transparency maintains engagement and motivation.

Celebrate implemented ideas. Recognize and reward team members whose ideas are put into action. This recognition reinforces the value of creativity and innovation.

Overcoming Creative Blocks

Creative blocks can hinder innovation. Identifying the root causes of these blocks is the first step to overcoming them. Is it due to stress, lack of inspiration, or something else?

Changing your environment can help. Rearrange your workspace, work from a new location, or take a walk outside. New surroundings can stimulate your senses and spark new ideas.

Taking breaks is also effective. Step away from the problem for a while. Engage in a different activity or take a holiday. This distance can provide a fresh perspective.

Engaging in creative activities outside of work can help too. Hobbies like painting, writing, or cooking can relax your mind and open new ways of thinking. These activities remind you that creativity is everywhere.

Collaborate with others to break through creative blocks. Discussing ideas with your team, peers, or mentors can provide new insights. Brainstorming sessions can generate fresh thinking.

Practice mindfulness and meditation to clear mental clutter. These practices reduce stress and improve focus. They create a mental space where new ideas can emerge.

Seek inspiration from diverse sources. Read books, explore art, travel, or look at other industries. New experiences can provide fresh perspectives and ideas.

Experiment with different creative techniques. Use mind mapping, SCAMPER, or the Six Thinking Hats. These tools can structure your thinking and boost creativity.

Set realistic expectations and embrace imperfection. Creative blocks often arise from the pressure to be perfect. Remember that ideas can be refined and improved over time.

SUSTAINING INNOVATION: KEEPING THE CREATIVE FLAME ALIVE

Sustaining innovation over the long term is essential. It requires consistent effort and the right environment. Here are some strategies to keep the creative flame alive.

Build a culture that values creativity. Encourage open communication and reward innovative ideas. Create a safe space where experimentation is encouraged and failure is seen as a learning opportunity.

Leadership plays a crucial role in sustaining innovation. Leaders should model and champion creative thinking. Provide the necessary resources for innovation, like time, funding, and training.

Continuously feed the creative pipeline. Stay updated on industry trends and technological advancements. Encourage team members to explore new ideas and stay curious.

Practice gratitude and positive thinking. Focus on the positive aspects of your journey and celebrate successes. This fosters a positive outlook and motivates continuous innovation.

Set realistic expectations and boundaries. Avoid burnout by knowing your limits and balancing work and personal life. This ensures you have the energy and focus to sustain creativity.

Embrace flexibility and openness to change. Be willing to pivot strategies and explore new ideas. This adaptability keeps your business agile and innovative.

Prudent financial planning is also important. Maintain a healthy cash flow and set aside reserves for tough times. Financial stability provides a buffer against uncertainties.

Implementing these strategies helps sustain innovation. They ensure that creativity remains a core part of your business. This continuous innovation drives growth and keeps your entrepreneurial journey dynamic and exciting.

CONCLUSION

Unlocking creative potential is essential for entrepreneurial success. By fostering an ideation-friendly environment, implementing regular brainstorming sessions, and encouraging cross-disciplinary collaboration, you can enhance creativity in your business. Practicing observational skills, leveraging creative thinking tools, and promoting continuous learning will keep the flow of innovation steady.

Encouraging individual creativity practices and embracing diverse perspectives enriches the overall creative process. Implementing idea management systems ensures that valuable ideas are captured and developed. Overcoming creative blocks and drawing inspiration from real-world case studies can keep your creative energy high.

Sustaining innovation requires a culture that values creativity, strong leadership, and continuous feeding of the creative pipeline. Practicing gratitude, setting realistic expectations, embracing flexibility, and prudent financial planning are all crucial. These strategies ensure that creativity and innovation remain integral to your business.

With these practices, you can unlock your creative potential, foster innovation, and drive success in your entrepreneurial journey.

Now that you have the tools to unlock and sustain creativity in your business, it's time to focus on how to communicate and sell your innovative ideas effectively. Creativity doesn't just stop at generating ideas, it's also about presenting them in a compelling way to your team, customers, and stakeholders.

In the next chapter, we will explore strategies for effective communication and persuasion, ensuring that your creative solutions gain the traction they deserve. By understanding how to articulate your vision and influence others, you will be better equipped to turn your innovative ideas into successful realities.

CHAPTER 6

WHAT SUCCESSFUL ENTREPRENEURS KNOW ABOUT CREATING A WINNING VISION

THE IMPORTANCE OF VISION

A clear vision is crucial for any entrepreneur. It shows what you want to achieve and helps guide your decisions. Your vision is a vivid picture of your future success. It inspires you and your team to keep moving forward.

A strong vision acts like a roadmap. It helps you navigate challenges and stay focused. When things get tough, your vision reminds you why you started. It keeps you motivated and determined.

Your vision isn't just for you. It's for your team and customers too. When everyone knows the vision, they can align their efforts. This creates a united front working towards the same goals.

CRAFTING YOUR VISION

Creating a vision starts with dreaming big. Think about what you want to achieve in the long run. Picture your business in five or ten years. Imagine the impact you want to make.

Write down your vision. Make it clear and specific. Use simple language so anyone can understand it. Avoid vague statements that can be misinterpreted.

Share your vision with your team. Get their input and buy-in. A shared vision is stronger and more motivating. It helps everyone feel invested in the success of the business.

Communicating Your Vision

Communicating your vision is key. Talk about it often and make it part of your daily operations. This keeps it fresh in everyone's mind.

Use various methods to share your vision. Hold meetings, send emails, and display it in your workspace. Consistent reminders reinforce its importance.

Lead by example. Show your commitment to the vision through your actions. When your team sees your dedication, they'll be more likely to follow.

Celebrate milestones that align with your vision. This shows progress and keeps the team motivated. It also reinforces the belief that the vision is achievable.

Setting SMART Goals

Goals turn your vision into action. They provide clear targets to aim for. Use the SMART framework to set effective goals. SMART stands for Specific, Measurable, Achievable, Relevant, and Time-bound.

Specific: Define clear and detailed objectives. Avoid vague statements.

Measurable: Set criteria for measuring progress. This helps track success and identify areas for improvement.

Achievable: Ensure goals are realistic. Setting impossible goals can lead to frustration and burnout.

Relevant: Align goals with your vision. Each goal should bring you closer to your long-term objectives.

Time-bound: Establish a timeline with deadlines. This creates urgency and keeps you focused.

Breaking Down Goals

Big goals can be overwhelming. Break them into smaller, manageable tasks. This makes them less intimidating and easier to tackle.

Create short-term objectives that lead to your long-term goals. Each small win builds momentum and confidence. Celebrate these achievements to keep motivation high.

Set milestones to track progress. Regular check-ins help ensure you're on the right path. Adjust your approach if needed to stay on track.

KEEPING GOALS FLEXIBLE

Flexibility is important in goal setting. Be prepared to adjust your goals as circumstances change. This doesn't mean giving up, but rather adapting to new challenges and opportunities.

Review your goals regularly. Check if they still align with your vision. Make changes if necessary to keep them relevant and achievable.

Stay open to feedback from your team. Their insights can help refine your goals and improve your approach. Collaborative goal setting creates a stronger, more committed team.

STAYING FOCUSED AND MOTIVATED

Staying focused on your goals is crucial. Distractions and setbacks are common, but don't let them derail you. Keep your vision in mind and stay committed.

Create a daily routine that prioritizes your goals. Consistent effort leads to steady progress. Avoid multitasking, which can reduce effectiveness.

Stay motivated by remembering why you set your goals. Reflect on your vision and the impact you want to make. This keeps you driven, even when the going gets tough.

Encourage your team to stay focused and motivated too. Recognize their efforts and celebrate their achievements. A motivated team is more productive and committed to success.

Using Tools and Techniques

Use tools and techniques to help achieve your goals. There are many resources available to assist with planning and tracking progress.

Project management software can organize tasks and deadlines. It helps keep everything on track and ensures nothing is forgotten.

Create to-do lists to prioritize daily tasks. This keeps you focused on what's important and helps manage time effectively.

Use calendars to schedule milestones and deadlines. Visual reminders keep you aware of upcoming targets and help maintain a sense of urgency.

Overcoming Obstacles

Obstacles are inevitable in any journey. Be prepared to face them and have strategies in place to overcome them.

Identify potential challenges in advance. This allows you to plan solutions and reduce their impact.

Stay resilient when facing setbacks. Remember that obstacles are temporary and can be overcome. Learn from these experiences and use them to grow stronger.

Seek support from your team and network. Collaborate to find solutions and share the burden. A united effort is often more effective.

EVALUATING AND ADJUSTING GOALS

Regular evaluation is crucial for success. Review your goals and progress frequently. This helps ensure you're on the right track and allows for adjustments.

Use metrics to measure progress. Data provides an objective view of your achievements and areas needing improvement.

Adjust goals as needed to stay aligned with your vision. Be flexible and open to change. Adaptability is key to long-term success.

Celebrate achievements to maintain motivation. Recognize progress and reward efforts. This reinforces the value of hard work and dedication.

REAL-WORLD EXAMPLES

Real-world examples make principles tangible. They show how others have succeeded and provide inspiration.

Consider Elon Musk's vision for SpaceX. He imagined making space travel accessible and sustainable. His clear vision guided every decision and inspired his team.

Think about Steve Jobs and Apple's vision. He wanted to create innovative products that changed the world. This vision drove the company's success and innovation.

Look at smaller businesses too. A local bakery might have a vision of becoming the community's favorite spot. Their goals and actions align with this vision, guiding their growth and success.

Practical Tips for Entrepreneurs

Start with a clear, specific vision. Write it down and share it with your team. Make it part of your daily operations.

Set SMART goals to turn your vision into action. Break them down into manageable tasks and set milestones.

Stay focused and motivated by remembering your vision. Create routines that prioritize your goals and use tools to track progress.

Be flexible and adjust goals as needed. Review progress regularly and make changes to stay aligned with your vision.

Overcome obstacles by planning ahead and staying resilient. Seek support from your team and network.

Evaluate and adjust goals to ensure success. Use metrics to measure progress and celebrate achievements.

Conclusion

A clear vision and effective goal setting are crucial for entrepreneurial success. They provide direction, motivation, and a roadmap to achieve your dreams.

By following these principles, you can turn your vision into reality. Set SMART goals, stay focused, and be flexible. Overcome obstacles and evaluate progress regularly.

Your vision is the foundation of your business. It inspires you and your team to strive for greatness. With clear goals and determination, you can achieve anything.

Remember, every successful entrepreneur started with a vision. They set goals, stayed focused, and adapted to challenges. You can do the same. Keep your vision clear, set your goals, and work towards your dreams every day.

With a clear vision and well-defined goals, you're now equipped to chart your path forward. Understanding your vision and setting goals gives you direction and purpose. But achieving success also requires making sound decisions.

Next, we'll delve into the critical skill of decision making. You'll learn to balance intuition with analysis, ensuring your choices are well-informed and aligned with your goals. By mastering decision making, you'll be better prepared to navigate the uncertainties of entrepreneurship and steer your business toward success. Let's explore how to make decisions that propel you forward.

CHAPTER 7

WHAT SUCCESSFUL ENTREPRENEURS KNOW ABOUT DECISION MAKING

Every day, entrepreneurs face choices that could make or break their business. How do they decide what to do? What secrets do they hold? In this chapter, we'll explore the art of decision-making through the eyes of successful entrepreneurs. We'll uncover how they handle uncertainty, learn from mistakes, and make confident choices that lead to success. By the end, you'll see decision-making not as a challenge, but as an opportunity for growth and innovation.

THE ART AND SCIENCE OF ENTREPRENEURIAL DECISION MAKING

Making decisions is a big part of being an entrepreneur. Good decisions can lead to success, while bad ones can cause problems. So, how do successful entrepreneurs make decisions? They use both their gut feelings and data.

Intuition, or gut feeling, comes from experience. It's like having a built-in guide. Data, on the other hand, is concrete. It provides facts and figures. Together, they help entrepreneurs make well-rounded choices.

But relying too much on one can be risky. Overthinking or doubting gut feelings can lead to missed opportunities. Ignoring data can result in poor decisions. The key is balance. Trust your instincts but back them up with facts.

For instance, an entrepreneur might feel that a new product will be a hit. They should still look at market research to confirm this feeling. This combination of intuition and data creates strong decision-making.

Embracing Uncertainty and Making Decisions with Incomplete Information

Entrepreneurs often must make decisions without all the facts. This uncertainty can be scary, but it's part of the job. Learning to embrace it is crucial.

When faced with incomplete information, successful entrepreneurs take calculated risks. They gather as much data as possible, but they don't wait for everything to be perfect. Waiting can mean missing out on big opportunities.

They also learn from their mistakes. Every decision, whether right or wrong, teaches something valuable. Mistakes aren't failures. They're lessons. This mindset helps entrepreneurs move forward even when things are unclear.

Imagine launching a new product without knowing if it will succeed. You gather data, ask for feedback, and monitor results. If it doesn't work, you learn and adjust. If it does, you capitalize on that success.

The Role of Experience and Continuous Learning

Experience plays a huge role in decision-making. The more you experience, the better your decisions become. Successful entrepreneurs use their past to guide their future.

But experience alone isn't enough. Continuous learning is just as important. Markets change, technologies evolve, and new challenges arise. Staying updated helps entrepreneurs make informed decisions.

Mentors can be a great source of learning. They offer insights from their own experiences. Reading industry news and attending workshops also keeps you in the loop. This ongoing education sharpens decision-making skills.

For example, a tech entrepreneur must stay updated on the latest trends. This knowledge helps them make decisions that keep their business competitive. Experience and learning go hand-in-hand to create a strong decision-maker.

The Importance of Speed and Decisiveness

Speed is crucial in the entrepreneurial world. Opportunities don't last forever. Being quick and decisive can make a big difference.

Hesitation can lead to missed chances. Successful entrepreneurs understand this. They act quickly but thoughtfully. They gather the necessary information and make swift decisions.

Confidence plays a big role here. Believing in your choices helps you act fast. Even if you're unsure, showing confidence can rally your team and keep things moving.

For instance, if a new market opens up, acting fast can secure a prime position. Waiting too long means competitors might take the lead. Speed and decisiveness help seize opportunities before they disappear.

The Power of Feedback in Decision Making

Feedback is a valuable tool for entrepreneurs. It provides different perspectives and can highlight blind spots. Successful entrepreneurs seek feedback regularly.

Feedback helps improve decisions. It can come from customers, employees, or mentors. Listening to others can provide insights you might have missed.

However, not all feedback is equal. It's important to weigh the source and relevance. Constructive feedback should be welcomed, while unhelpful criticism can be ignored.

For example, customer feedback can reveal if a product needs tweaking. Employee feedback can improve internal processes. By valuing feedback, entrepreneurs make better-informed decisions.

Building Confidence in Your Decisions

Confidence in decision-making is essential. It keeps you focused and motivated. Without it, doubt can creep in and derail your plans.

Successful entrepreneurs build confidence through preparation and practice. They do their homework and trust their instincts. Each decision, successful or not, builds more confidence.

Practice also helps. The more decisions you make, the better you get. It's like a muscle that gets stronger with use. Reflecting on past decisions and learning from them also boosts confidence.

For instance, a startup founder who confidently pitches their idea to investors is more likely to succeed. Confidence shows you believe in your vision and can convince others to believe in it too.

The Impact of Team Decision Making

Decisions don't have to be made alone. Successful entrepreneurs often rely on their teams. Team decision-making can bring in diverse perspectives and ideas.

Collaboration can lead to better outcomes. It combines the strengths and knowledge of different people. When everyone contributes, the decision is more well-rounded.

But it's important to manage this process well. Clear communication and a structured approach are key. Everyone should have a chance to share their views, but the final decision should be clear.

For example, in a product development meeting, different team members bring unique insights. Marketing, sales, and design all have valuable input. Together, they make a decision that's best for the product and company.

Overcoming Fear of Making Wrong Decisions

Fear of making wrong decisions can paralyze an entrepreneur. It's natural to worry about the consequences, but it's important not to let fear stop you.

Successful entrepreneurs understand that making mistakes is part of the journey. They accept that not every decision will be perfect. What matters is how they handle mistakes and learn from them.

To overcome this fear, focus on the bigger picture. Remember that one wrong decision doesn't define your success. Stay flexible and be ready to adapt if things go wrong.

For instance, if a marketing campaign fails, analyze what went wrong. Use this knowledge to improve future campaigns. Don't let the fear of failure hold you back.

The Role of Ethics in Decision Making

Ethical decision-making is crucial for long-term success. Entrepreneurs must consider the impact of their choices on others.

Making ethical decisions builds trust with customers, employees, and partners. It enhances your reputation and fosters loyalty. People want to support businesses they believe in.

Successful entrepreneurs weigh the ethical implications of their decisions. They ask themselves if their choices are fair and just. This approach not only avoids potential problems but also creates a positive business environment.

For example, choosing to use sustainable materials in products might cost more initially. But it builds a brand that's respected for its values. Ethical decisions pay off in the long run.

THE BENEFITS OF REFLECTING ON DECISIONS

Reflection is a powerful tool in decision-making. Taking time to look back at past decisions helps improve future ones.

Successful entrepreneurs make reflection a regular practice. They analyze what worked, what didn't, and why. This continuous improvement process sharpens their decision-making skills.

Reflection helps identify patterns and areas for growth. It also reinforces good practices and highlights mistakes to avoid. Writing down reflections can be particularly effective.

For instance, after a major project, reflect on the process. What went well? What could have been better? Use these insights to make the next project even more successful.

LEVERAGING TECHNOLOGY IN DECISION MAKING

Technology can significantly enhance decision-making. Tools like data analytics and AI provide valuable insights.

Successful entrepreneurs use technology to gather and analyze data. This helps them make more informed decisions. It also saves time and reduces the risk of errors.

For example, a retail business might use analytics to understand customer behavior. This data helps make decisions about inventory, marketing, and product development.

However, it's important to remember that technology is a tool, not a replacement for human judgment. Use it to support your decisions, not make them for you.

ADAPTING DECISION-MAKING STYLES

Different situations require different decision-making styles. Successful entrepreneurs adapt their approach based on the context.

For quick, low-risk decisions, a more intuitive approach might work best. For complex, high-stakes decisions, a detailed analysis is needed.

Being flexible in your decision-making style ensures you respond appropriately to each situation. It also helps in managing different types of challenges effectively.

For instance, deciding on a marketing slogan might be a quick, creative decision. Launching a new product line requires thorough research and planning. Adapting your style to fit the situation leads to better outcomes.

BUILDING A DECISION-MAKING FRAMEWORK

Having a framework for decision-making can be very helpful. It provides a consistent approach and ensures nothing is overlooked.

A good framework includes defining the problem, gathering information, exploring options, making the decision, and reviewing the outcome. This structured approach simplifies complex decisions.

Successful entrepreneurs often develop their own frameworks. They tailor them to fit their specific needs and preferences. This personalized approach makes decision-making more efficient.

For example, an entrepreneur might use a framework that includes a checklist for key considerations. This ensures all important factors are addressed before making a final decision.

The Impact of Culture on Decision Making

Company culture influences decision-making. A supportive, open culture encourages better decisions.

Successful entrepreneurs build a culture that values input from everyone. They foster an environment where ideas can be freely shared and discussed.

This inclusive culture leads to more innovative solutions. It also boosts morale and engagement among team members.

For instance, a tech company with an open culture might hold regular brainstorming sessions. This allows employees to contribute ideas, leading to more creative and effective solutions.

Trusting Your Team in Decision Making

Trust is crucial in team decision-making. Successful entrepreneurs trust their team members' expertise and judgment.

Delegating decisions to the right people empowers them and leverages their skills. It also frees up the entrepreneur to focus on bigger strategic issues.

However, trust doesn't mean lack of oversight. Regular check-ins and feedback ensure alignment and accountability.

For example, entrusting the marketing team with campaign decisions shows confidence in their abilities. Regular updates and reviews ensure the campaign aligns with the company's goals.

The Role of Vision in Decision Making

A clear vision guides decision-making. Successful entrepreneurs have a strong vision for their business.

This vision acts as a compass, helping them make choices that align with their goals. It provides direction and purpose.

When faced with decisions, they ask how it fits with their vision. This keeps them focused and consistent in their approach.

For instance, if an entrepreneur's vision is to create sustainable products, they will prioritize eco-friendly options. This vision-driven decision-making ensures every choice supports their long-term goals.

Handling Unpopular Decisions

Not all decisions will be popular. Sometimes, tough choices are necessary for the greater good.

Successful entrepreneurs handle unpopular decisions with transparency and empathy. They communicate the reasons clearly and listen to feedback.

Being open about the decision process helps build trust, even if people disagree. It's important to stand firm but also be willing to address concerns.

For example, cutting costs might require layoffs. Explaining the reasons and offering support can help manage the impact and maintain trust.

The Benefits of Long-Term Thinking

Long-term thinking is essential in decision-making. It helps entrepreneurs stay focused on their ultimate goals.

Successful entrepreneurs balance short-term needs with long-term vision. They make decisions that build sustainable success.

This approach avoids quick fixes that might cause problems later. It ensures the business grows steadily and healthily.

For instance, investing in quality products might cost more now but pays off in customer loyalty. Long-term thinking creates a strong foundation for future success.

Learning from Other Entrepreneurs

Learning from others is invaluable. Successful entrepreneurs study how others make decisions.

They read biographies, attend talks, and seek mentors. This broadens their perspective and provides new ideas.

Analyzing others' successes and failures offers practical insights. It helps avoid common pitfalls and adopt best practices.

For example, reading about how Steve Jobs made product decisions can inspire better decision-making. Learning from others accelerates growth and improves skills.

The Importance of Passion in Decision Making

Passion fuels decision-making. Successful entrepreneurs are passionate about their work.

This passion drives them to make bold, confident decisions. It keeps them motivated even in tough times.

Passion also inspires others. It creates a positive energy that influences the whole team.

For instance, an entrepreneur passionate about innovation will push for creative solutions. This passion creates a dynamic, forward-thinking company culture.

By incorporating these strategies, you can enhance your decision-making skills and invigorate your entrepreneurial journey. Remember, good decision-making is a skill that grows with practice and reflection. Keep learning, stay flexible, and trust your instincts.

CONCLUSION

Decision-making is the backbone of entrepreneurial success. Throughout this chapter, we've uncovered the methods that successful entrepreneurs use to navigate the complexities of their choices. By balancing intuition with data, embracing uncertainty, learning continuously, and acting decisively, they turn potential obstacles into opportunities. Remember, each decision is an opportunity to grow, innovate, and move closer to your goals. Armed with these insights, you're not just ready to make decisions—you're ready to make the right ones. Your journey to entrepreneurial success is paved with the choices you make, and now you have the tools to make them count.

You've just discovered the secrets of making sound decisions as an entrepreneur. Now, let's take it a step further. In the next chapter, we'll explore the powerful networking strategies used by successful entrepreneurs. You'll learn how to build meaningful connections that go beyond exchanging business cards, creating opportunities for growth and collaboration. Get ready to dive into the art of networking and see how it can transform your entrepreneurial journey.

CHAPTER 8

THE GAME-CHANGING NETWORKING TIPS FROM SUCCESSFUL ENTREPRENEURS

Imagine standing in a room filled with potential partners, mentors, and friends. Networking isn't just about swapping business cards. It's about forming meaningful connections that can transform your entrepreneurial journey. This chapter will guide you through the art of effective networking, sharing insights from successful entrepreneurs who have mastered this skill.

NETWORKING IS MORE THAN JUST EXCHANGING BUSINESS CARDS

Networking in entrepreneurship goes beyond the simple exchange of business cards and contacts. True networking is about building meaningful relationships that lead to growth, opportunities, and personal development.

REDEFINING NETWORKING

Think of networking not as a crowded room where business cards are exchanged but as a community where each relationship is a potential partnership. Entrepreneurs should aim to create connections based on respect, shared interests, and genuine interactions. The value of a network lies in its relevance and depth, not just its size.

To redefine your approach to networking, focus on quality over quantity. Spend time getting to know a few people well rather than trying to meet everyone at an event. Follow up with those you meet and build on the initial connection. Remember, a small, strong network can be more valuable than a large, superficial one.

MULTI-DIMENSIONAL BENEFITS

Networking offers more than just immediate business opportunities. A strong network can provide ideas, advice, mentorship, and support. It can lead to collaborations, partnerships, and entry into new markets. Personally, a robust network serves as a sounding board for ideas, a support system during challenges, and a source of inspiration.

For example, consider joining industry-specific groups or communities where you can share knowledge and learn from others. These groups can become valuable resources for problem-solving and innovation. Regularly attending meetups, conferences, and workshops can also keep you connected and informed about industry trends.

AUTHENTICITY IN NETWORKING

Authenticity is key in today's networking landscape. Engage with others out of genuine interest, not just to see what you can gain. Share your passions and challenges, and listen to others with the intent to understand. Authentic networking creates connections that are professionally beneficial and personally enriching.

To practice authenticity, be honest about your experiences and goals. People appreciate transparency and are more likely to trust and support you. Avoid trying to impress others with exaggerated claims. Instead, focus on building real relationships based on mutual respect and interest.

BUILDING A DIVERSE NETWORK

A diverse network is invaluable. Connect with people from various industries, backgrounds, and perspectives. Diversity enriches your network, offering a range of viewpoints and experiences. It challenges you to think differently, exposes you to new ideas, and fosters creativity and innovation.

Seek out networking opportunities outside your usual circles. Attend events that attract different types of professionals, or join groups focused on issues or industries you're less familiar with. This approach broadens your horizons and helps you build a network that's rich in diverse experiences and insights.

Nurturing Relationships

Networking is a continuous process. Follow up, stay in touch, and offer help and support. Relationships need regular care to grow. Simple gestures like sharing an article of interest, congratulating a contact on an achievement, or checking in can go a long way.

Set aside time each week to reach out to your network. Schedule coffee meetings, phone calls, or video chats to catch up. These efforts demonstrate that you value the relationship and are committed to maintaining it. Over time, these small acts of engagement build strong, lasting connections.

Leveraging Networks for Opportunities

A well-nurtured network is a source of opportunities. Be proactive in reaching out, discussing ideas, and exploring potential synergies. Act as a connector by introducing contacts who might benefit from knowing each other.

For instance, if you know two people who could collaborate on a project, introduce them to each other. This not only helps them but also positions you as a valuable connector within your network. By facilitating connections, you strengthen your own relationships and create a network that's actively engaged and supportive.

Personal Development through Networking

Networking plays a crucial role in personal development. It exposes you to different leadership styles, business strategies, and life philosophies. Engaging with a diverse network can accelerate your personal growth, broaden your horizons, and deepen your understanding of the business world and yourself.

Use your network to seek mentorship and advice. Identify individuals whose careers or achievements you admire and reach out to them for guidance. Learning from their experiences can provide valuable insights and help you navigate your own entrepreneurial journey more effectively.

Strategic Networking

Strategic networking isn't just about socializing at events. It's a deliberate process of identifying and engaging with individuals who can significantly impact your business success.

Identifying Key Contacts

To identify key contacts, understand your business goals and the gaps in your knowledge or network. Key contacts might be industry veterans with valuable insights, potential partners with complementary skills, or influencers who can introduce you to larger audiences.

Make a list of the types of people who could help you achieve your goals. Then, research where these individuals are likely to be found. This could be specific industry events, professional associations, or online communities. Being intentional about where you spend your networking efforts increases the likelihood of meeting valuable contacts.

Crafting Engagement Strategies

Once you've identified key individuals, craft a strategy to engage with them. This isn't about bombarding them with requests but building a connection based on mutual interest and respect. Start with a simple, personalized introduction that shows genuine interest in their work.

For example, when reaching out via email or LinkedIn, reference something specific they've done that you admire or find interesting. This shows that you've done your homework and are sincerely interested in them as a person, not just what they can do for you.

Networking Events

At networking events, focus on targeted conversations rather than just handing out business cards. Listen as much as you talk, understand the other person's interests and needs, and find common ground. Memorable conversations often happen in casual settings, not just during formal presentations.

Prepare a few questions or topics in advance to help guide your conversations. This preparation can make you feel more confident and ensure that you make the most of each interaction. Follow up with a personalized message after the event to reinforce the connection and keep the conversation going.

Leveraging Social Media

Social media and online platforms are powerful tools for strategic networking. They allow you to connect with key contacts who might be geographically distant. Engage with their content, contribute to discussions, and share relevant information to build a virtual relationship.

Regularly share your own insights and updates to stay visible and relevant. Participate in online discussions and groups related to your industry. This consistent presence helps you build a robust online network and can lead to meaningful offline connections.

Networking Skills

Networking skills are essential for effective relationship-building in entrepreneurship. This section focuses on communication and social intelligence – the skills that make networking engaging and fruitful.

Effective Communication

Effective communication is the cornerstone of networking. It's about conveying ideas clearly and resonantly. Entrepreneurs need to be adept storytellers, capable of articulating their visions, challenges, and successes in an engaging manner.

Practice your pitch so you can clearly and concisely explain what you do and why it matters. Tailor your message to different audiences, highlighting aspects that will resonate most with each person. Storytelling is a powerful tool – use it to make your points memorable and engaging.

Social Intelligence

Social intelligence helps navigate the dynamics of networking interactions. It involves reading the room, understanding social cues, and adapting your approach accordingly. This intelligence is crucial for building rapport and trust.

Pay attention to body language, tone of voice, and other non-verbal cues during conversations. These signals can provide insight into how the other person is feeling and how best to engage with them. Being aware of these cues helps you adjust your communication style to suit the situation.

ACTIVE LISTENING

Active listening is a powerful networking skill. It involves genuinely tuning into what others are saying, showing empathy, and understanding their perspectives. This transforms conversations into meaningful exchanges.

Practice active listening by focusing on the speaker, avoiding interruptions, and responding thoughtfully. Summarize what you've heard to show understanding and ask follow-up questions that demonstrate genuine interest. This approach builds trust and makes the other person feel valued.

POSITIVE FIRST IMPRESSIONS

First impressions set the tone for future interactions. A positive first impression involves confident body language, proper attire, and a warm, genuine smile. Projecting approachability and professionalism opens doors to fruitful interactions.

Pay attention to your appearance and body language. Dress appropriately for the occasion and ensure your posture and expressions convey confidence and openness. A strong handshake, eye contact, and a smile can go a long way in making a positive impression.

RECIPROCITY IN RELATIONSHIPS

Reciprocity is at the heart of successful networking. It's about creating a balance where both parties feel valued and supported.

Offering Help

One effective way to build a network is to offer help. This could be sharing expertise, making introductions, or providing feedback. Helping without immediate expectation of return sets a foundation of goodwill and generosity.

For instance, if a contact is looking for a resource or connection you can provide, offer it willingly. This gesture shows you're willing to support others and builds a positive reputation within your network.

Building Trust

Genuine reciprocity builds trust, a cornerstone of strong relationships. Trust evolves when people see that you're willing to contribute to the relationship, not just take from it.

Follow through on promises and be reliable. Small actions, like responding promptly to messages or keeping commitments, build a foundation of trust over time. Trustworthy behavior encourages others to reciprocate and strengthens the overall relationship.

Balanced Relationships

While giving is essential, so is the ability to receive. A relationship where one party constantly gives and the other takes is unsustainable. Be open to accepting help, advice, and support when offered.

If someone offers assistance, accept it graciously and look for ways to reciprocate. This balance ensures that both parties feel valued and the relationship remains mutually beneficial.

Expanding Your Network Beyond the Comfort Zone

Expanding your network beyond your comfort zone can bring new perspectives, opportunities, and valuable lessons.

Stepping into the Unfamiliar

Venturing beyond your usual circle of peers can open up new opportunities. Attend events and join groups that might not align directly with your business but offer exposure to different industries, cultures, and backgrounds.

Explore events and communities outside your immediate field. These environments can introduce you to innovative ideas and different ways of thinking that can benefit your business.

Cross-Cultural Networking

Cross-cultural networking involves understanding and appreciating different cultural perspectives. It requires curiosity, respect, and a willingness to learn about different business etiquettes and traditions.

Approach cross-cultural interactions with an open mind and a respectful attitude. Learn about different cultures and practices to better engage with diverse contacts. This understanding fosters deeper connections and can open doors to international opportunities.

Leveraging Digital Platforms

Online platforms make expanding your network more accessible. Engage in online forums, social media groups, and virtual conferences to connect with people across the globe. The digital world offers endless opportunities for networking.

Participate actively in online communities related to your industry. Share valuable content, engage in discussions, and build a presence that attracts a diverse audience. Online networking can complement your in-person efforts and expand your reach.

Conclusion

Networking is a multifaceted skill that extends beyond mere socializing. Successful entrepreneurs understand the power of building meaningful, reciprocal relationships. By strategically engaging with key contacts, mastering communication and social intelligence, and expanding their networks beyond comfort zones, they create a dynamic web of connections that foster growth, innovation, and personal development. As you apply these game-changing networking tips, you'll see your entrepreneurial journey enriched with new opportunities and lasting relationships.

You've mastered the art of networking and relationship building. Now, it's time to explore another crucial element of entrepreneurial success. In the next chapter, we'll delve into how mindfulness can boost your business. Discover how mindfulness enhances focus, reduces stress, and sharpens decision-making. Get ready to learn practical mindfulness techniques that will help you stay calm and clear-headed, even in the face of challenges. This journey into mindfulness will not only improve your mental and emotional well-being but also provide a powerful edge in your entrepreneurial endeavors.

CHAPTER 9

HOW SUCCESSFUL ENTREPRENEURS USE MINDFULNESS TO BOOST THEIR BUSINESS

Imagine starting your day with a clear, focused mind, ready to tackle any challenge that comes your way. Picture making decisions with confidence, feeling calm under pressure, and maintaining your productivity without burning out. Sounds like a dream, right? This is the reality for many successful entrepreneurs who have discovered the secret weapon to thriving in the fast-paced business world: mindfulness.

In this chapter, we'll explore how mindfulness can transform your entrepreneurial journey. You'll learn practical techniques to reduce stress, improve focus, and enhance decision-making. We'll also share insights from top entrepreneurs who credit mindfulness for their success. Get ready to unlock the power of mindfulness and take your business to the next level.

The Importance of Mindfulness in Entrepreneurship

Mindfulness is a powerful tool for entrepreneurs. It helps reduce stress, improve focus, and make better decisions. Many successful entrepreneurs use mindfulness daily.

Mindfulness means being fully present in the moment. This helps you notice your thoughts and feelings without getting overwhelmed. For entrepreneurs, this is crucial because it helps manage the constant pressures and challenges they face.

Enhancing Focus and Clarity

Mindfulness improves focus. It reduces distractions and helps you concentrate on the task at hand. This is especially important for entrepreneurs juggling multiple responsibilities.

When you practice mindfulness, you train your brain to stay on track. This means fewer interruptions and more productivity. You get more done in less time.

To improve focus, start with simple breathing exercises. Sit comfortably, close your eyes, and take deep breaths. Focus on your breath going in and out. Do this for a few minutes each day.

Using mindfulness apps can also help. Apps like Headspace or Calm guide you through mindfulness exercises and remind you to take breaks. These tools help keep your mind sharp and your productivity high.

ALLEVIATING STRESS

Entrepreneurship is stressful. There are constant pressures and challenges. Mindfulness can help manage this stress effectively.

Mindfulness teaches you to stay calm in tough situations. It helps you see things more clearly and respond thoughtfully. This reduces stress and makes you more resilient.

To start, try a few minutes of meditation each day. Sit quietly, close your eyes, and focus on your breath. When your mind wanders, gently bring it back to your breath. This practice can significantly reduce stress over time.

Regular practice can lead to better health and well-being. You'll feel better, think more clearly, and make better decisions. Mindfulness helps you achieve this balance.

DECISION MAKING WITH A CLEAR MIND

Clear decision-making is key for entrepreneurs. Mindfulness helps clear your mind and make better choices. When you are calm and focused, you can think more clearly.

Before making a decision, take a few deep breaths. This helps calm your mind and focus on the present moment. You'll make better choices with a clear mind.

Mindfulness also helps you stay present. When you're fully engaged in the moment, you can weigh your options more effectively. This leads to better decisions.

Regular mindfulness practice improves overall clarity. It helps you stay focused and think more clearly. This is crucial for making good business decisions.

Examples of Mindfulness

Many successful entrepreneurs use mindfulness. For example, Steve Jobs practiced mindfulness regularly. He credited it with helping him stay focused and creative.

Arianna Huffington also practices mindfulness. She uses it to manage stress and stay productive. Her company, Thrive Global, promotes mindfulness in the workplace.

Marc Benioff, CEO of Salesforce, is another example. He incorporates mindfulness into his daily routine. This helps him stay calm and focused in his demanding role.

These examples show the benefits of mindfulness. It helps entrepreneurs manage stress, improve focus, and make better decisions.

Implementing Mindfulness in Your Routine

Start small. You don't need to spend hours meditating. Even a few minutes each day can make a big difference.

Begin with simple breathing exercises. Take deep breaths and focus on your breath. This helps calm your mind and improve focus.

Use mindfulness apps for guided exercises. These apps provide easy-to-follow instructions and reminders. They help you stay on track with your practice.

Set aside a few minutes each day for mindfulness. Make it a part of your daily routine. This consistency will help you see the benefits over time.

Benefits of Mindfulness

Mindfulness has many benefits. It reduces stress, improves focus, and enhances decision-making. These are all crucial for successful entrepreneurship.

Reduced stress leads to better health and well-being. You'll feel better and have more energy to tackle challenges. This is essential for long-term success.

Improved focus means better productivity. You'll get more done in less time. This helps you stay ahead in your business.

Better decision-making leads to better outcomes. When you think clearly, you make better choices. This is crucial for growing your business.

Mindfulness Exercises

There are many mindfulness exercises you can try. Breathing exercises are a good start. Focus on your breath for a few minutes each day.

Meditation is another effective practice. Sit quietly and focus on your breath. When your mind wanders, gently bring it back to your breath.

Mindfulness apps offer guided exercises. These apps provide instructions and reminders. They help you stay consistent with your practice.

Try different exercises to see what works best for you. The key is to practice regularly and make mindfulness a part of your daily routine.

Overcoming Challenges

Starting a mindfulness practice can be challenging. It takes time and patience. But the benefits are worth the effort.

One common challenge is finding time. Start with just a few minutes each day. Gradually increase the time as you get more comfortable.

Another challenge is staying consistent. Use reminders and apps to help you stay on track. Make mindfulness a priority in your daily routine.

It's also important to be patient. Mindfulness takes time to develop. Stick with it and you'll see the benefits over time.

Integrating Mindfulness into Work

Integrating mindfulness into your work routine can enhance its benefits. Start meetings with a few minutes of deep breathing to center everyone's focus. This practice can improve the quality of discussions and decisions.

Encourage mindful breaks throughout the day. Short breaks to focus on breathing or stretching can help maintain productivity and reduce stress. This practice keeps you and your team refreshed.

Use mindfulness during challenging tasks. When facing a difficult project, take a moment to breathe deeply and focus your mind. This can help you approach the task with a clear and calm mindset.

Promote a mindful work culture. Encourage your team to practice mindfulness. Provide resources and support for those interested. A mindful team is often more productive and cohesive.

Long-Term Benefits of Mindfulness

The long-term benefits of mindfulness are significant. Over time, you'll notice improved mental clarity and reduced stress. This leads to better overall health and well-being.

Mindfulness can enhance your leadership skills. A clear and calm mind makes you a more effective leader. You'll make better decisions and handle challenges more gracefully.

A mindful approach to work can lead to innovation. When your mind is clear, you're more open to new ideas and creative solutions. This can drive your business forward.

Mindfulness also fosters resilience. It helps you bounce back from setbacks and stay focused on your goals. This is crucial for long-term success in entrepreneurship.

CONCLUSION

Mindfulness is a powerful tool for entrepreneurs. It helps reduce stress, improve focus, and make better decisions. By incorporating mindfulness into your daily routine, you can boost your business and improve your well-being.

Start small and be consistent. Use breathing exercises, meditation, and mindfulness apps. Make mindfulness a part of your daily routine.

Learn from successful entrepreneurs who practice mindfulness. Follow their examples and see how mindfulness can benefit your business.

Mindfulness can transform your entrepreneurial journey. It helps you stay calm, focused, and clear-headed. This leads to better decisions and greater success.

Incorporate mindfulness into your life and experience the benefits. Your business and well-being will improve, leading to a more successful and fulfilling entrepreneurial journey.

CHAPTER 10

THE ADAPTABILITY SECRETS OF HIGHLY SUCCESSFUL ENTREPRENEURS

In the fast-paced world of business, change is constant. Successful entrepreneurs must adapt quickly to survive and thrive. Adaptability means more than just reacting to change; it means embracing and anticipating it. This chapter will explore how entrepreneurs can develop and use adaptability to their advantage, with practical advice and real-world examples.

THE ESSENCE OF ADAPTABILITY IN ENTREPRENEURSHIP

Adaptability is crucial for entrepreneurs. It involves being open to new ideas, willing to change course, and ready to seize opportunities. Entrepreneurs who embrace adaptability can navigate challenges and stay competitive. This section will explain why adaptability is essential and how it can benefit your business.

Adaptable entrepreneurs don't fear change. They see it as an opportunity to grow. By staying flexible, they can respond quickly to market shifts. This keeps their businesses relevant and resilient.

To become more adaptable, start by embracing a growth mindset. Believe that you can learn and improve over time. This mindset helps you stay open to new ideas and willing to try new approaches.

Flexibility: More Than Just Bending

Flexibility is a key part of adaptability. It means being able to change plans when needed. Flexibility is about thoughtful pivoting, not just bending to circumstances.

To develop flexibility, practice questioning old methods. Ask yourself if there's a better way to do things. This helps you stay innovative and open to improvement.

Agile methodologies can help foster flexibility. These are frameworks that encourage rapid changes and continuous improvement. They help teams stay adaptable and responsive. For example, the Scrum framework allows for regular adjustments based on feedback and new information.

Innovation frameworks like Design Thinking can also support flexibility. These frameworks encourage creative problem-solving and user-centered design. They help you develop new solutions quickly. Design Thinking involves empathizing with users, defining problems, ideating solutions, prototyping, and testing.

Proactive Adaptation: Anticipating Change

Being proactive means anticipating change before it happens. This helps you stay ahead of the curve. Proactive adaptation involves staying attuned to market trends, customer feedback, and technological advancements.

To anticipate change, keep a close eye on industry trends. Follow news and updates in your field. This helps you spot emerging opportunities and threats. Use tools like Google Alerts or industry newsletters to stay informed.

Customer feedback is another valuable source of information. Regularly ask your customers for their opinions. Use their feedback to guide your decisions and improvements. Conduct surveys, hold focus groups, and read online reviews to gather insights.

Technological advancements can also drive change. Stay informed about new tools and technologies in your industry. These can offer new ways to improve your business. Attend industry conferences, participate in webinars, and network with tech-savvy peers.

The Art of the Pivot

Pivoting means making significant changes when the current strategy isn't working. This can be risky, but it's often necessary for growth. Successful pivots can open new paths to success.

To execute a pivot, start by analyzing your current situation. Identify what's not working and why. This helps you understand where changes are needed. Use SWOT analysis (Strengths, Weaknesses, Opportunities, Threats) to assess your situation.

Next, develop a new strategy. This should be based on your analysis and guided by your long-term goals. Make sure your team understands and supports the new direction. Communicate the reasons for the pivot and how it aligns with your vision.

Implement the pivot step-by-step. Start with small changes and test their impact. This helps you manage risks and adjust as needed. Use A/B testing to compare new strategies with old ones and gather data to inform decisions.

Successful pivots require flexibility and open communication. Keep your team informed and involved. This ensures everyone is aligned and committed to the new strategy. Hold regular meetings to discuss progress and address any concerns.

EMBRACING NEW TECHNOLOGIES

Technology is a key driver of change in business. Embracing new technologies can help you stay competitive and innovative. This section will explore how to identify and integrate new tools into your business.

Start by identifying technologies that can benefit your business. Look for tools that improve efficiency, enhance customer experience, or open new markets. Research and test these technologies to see how they fit your needs. Use platforms like G2 or Capterra to compare software options.

Once you've identified useful technologies, develop a plan to integrate them. This should include training for your team and adjustments to your processes. Ensure everyone understands how to use the new tools and why they're important. Create a timeline for implementation and set clear goals for what you hope to achieve.

Monitor the impact of new technologies on your business. Track key metrics to see how they improve performance. Use this data to make informed decisions about future technology investments. Tools like Google Analytics or CRM systems can help you track performance and gather insights.

Examples of Adaptability

Many successful entrepreneurs have demonstrated adaptability. These examples show how flexibility, proactive adaptation, and technology integration can lead to success.

Steve Jobs is a prime example. He led Apple through multiple pivots, including the shift from computers to mobile devices. His ability to anticipate change and embrace new technologies kept Apple at the forefront of innovation.

Another example is Reed Hastings of Netflix. He pivoted the company from DVD rentals to streaming, anticipating changes in how people consume media. This proactive adaptation helped Netflix become a leader in the entertainment industry.

Sara Blakely, founder of Spanx, also shows adaptability. She used customer feedback to continuously improve her products. This flexibility helped her create a brand that meets customer needs and stays ahead of competitors.

These examples highlight the importance of adaptability in entrepreneurship. By being flexible, proactive, and tech-savvy, you can navigate challenges and seize opportunities.

Implementing Adaptability in Your Business

Developing adaptability requires practice and commitment. Here are practical steps to help you implement adaptability in your business.

First, foster a culture of flexibility. Encourage your team to question old methods and suggest new ideas. This keeps your business innovative and responsive. Create an open environment where feedback is valued.

Next, stay informed about industry trends and customer feedback. Use this information to guide your decisions and anticipate change. This helps you stay ahead of the curve. Regularly share insights with your team and discuss potential impacts.

Embrace new technologies that can improve your business. Identify, test, and integrate useful tools. This keeps your operations efficient and competitive. Allocate resources for training and support to ensure smooth adoption.

Finally, be prepared to pivot when needed. Regularly assess your strategies and be willing to make changes. This helps you stay aligned with your goals and adapt to new challenges. Set up a process for evaluating and implementing pivots.

Benefits of Adaptability

Adaptability offers many benefits for entrepreneurs. It helps you navigate challenges, seize opportunities, and stay competitive. This section will explore these benefits in detail.

One key benefit is resilience. Adaptable businesses can withstand changes and bounce back from setbacks. This keeps them strong and stable.

Adaptability also drives innovation. By staying open to new ideas and technologies, you can develop creative solutions. This helps you stay ahead of competitors.

Improved decision-making is another benefit. Adaptable entrepreneurs can respond quickly to changes. This helps them make better decisions and take advantage of opportunities.

Finally, adaptability enhances customer satisfaction. By listening to customer feedback and making improvements, you can better meet their needs. This builds loyalty and trust.

Overcoming Challenges to Adaptability

Developing adaptability can be challenging. It requires a willingness to change and take risks. This section will explore common challenges and how to overcome them.

One challenge is resistance to change. People often prefer familiar routines. To overcome this, communicate the benefits of adaptability. Show how it can lead to growth and success. Use examples and data to support your message.

Another challenge is fear of failure. Pivoting and trying new ideas can be risky. To manage this, start with small changes and test their impact. This helps you manage risks and build confidence. Celebrate small wins to encourage a positive mindset.

Lack of information can also hinder adaptability. To stay informed, regularly gather data on industry trends and customer feedback. Use this information to guide your decisions. Set up systems for continuous learning and improvement.

Finally, integrating new technologies can be challenging. Ensure your team is trained and supported. This helps them embrace new tools and use them effectively. Provide ongoing training and resources to address any issues.

CONCLUSION

Adaptability is a crucial trait for successful entrepreneurs. It involves being flexible, proactive, and open to new technologies. By developing adaptability, you can navigate challenges and seize opportunities.

Start by fostering a culture of flexibility in your business. Stay informed about industry trends and customer feedback. Embrace new technologies and be prepared to pivot when needed.

Learn from successful entrepreneurs who demonstrate adaptability. Follow their examples and see how flexibility, proactive adaptation, and technology integration can benefit your business.

Developing adaptability takes practice and commitment. But the benefits—resilience, innovation, better decision-making, and enhanced customer satisfaction—are well worth the effort.

Embrace adaptability and take your entrepreneurial journey to the next level. Your business will be better prepared to face challenges and seize opportunities, leading to long-term success.

CHAPTER 11

MASTER THE COMPLETE BLUEPRINT OF SUCCESSFUL ENTREPRENEURS

Being a successful entrepreneur involves more than just having a great idea. It requires constant growth, self-awareness, and the ability to adapt. This chapter will guide you through essential steps to master the complete blueprint of successful entrepreneurs. We'll cover self-assessment, creating a growth plan, practical exercises, daily practices, seeking feedback, and continuous learning.

SELF-ASSESSMENT: IDENTIFYING YOUR ENTREPRENEURIAL STRENGTHS AND AREAS FOR GROWTH

Self-awareness is crucial for entrepreneurs. Knowing your strengths and weaknesses helps you make better decisions and plans. Start by taking personality tests like Myers-Briggs or the Big Five. These tests can give you insights into your traits and behaviors.

Use a SWOT analysis to evaluate your Strengths, Weaknesses, Opportunities, and Threats. Write down your strengths and weaknesses. Identify opportunities that can help you grow and threats that might hinder your progress. This analysis provides a clear picture of where you stand and where you need to improve.

Tools and Techniques for Comprehensive Self-Evaluation

Several tools can help you understand yourself better. The Myers-Briggs Type Indicator (MBTI) categorizes you into one of 16 personality types. It can help you understand how you make decisions and interact with others. The Big Five Personality Test measures five key traits: openness, conscientiousness, extraversion, agreeableness, and neuroticism. This test gives you a broader view of your personality.

Another useful tool is 360-degree feedback. This involves getting feedback from your peers, employees, and supervisors. It provides a well-rounded view of your strengths and areas for improvement. To make the most of these tools, take the tests seriously and reflect on the results.

Creating a Personalized Growth Plan

Once you've assessed yourself, create a growth plan. Start by setting realistic and measurable goals. These goals should be specific, achievable, and time-bound. For example, if you want to improve your leadership skills, set a goal to complete a leadership course within three months.

Next, outline the steps you need to take to achieve these goals. Break your goals into smaller tasks. For instance, if your goal is to learn digital marketing, your tasks might include reading a book on the subject, taking an online course, and applying what you've learned to a project. Monitor your progress regularly and adjust your plan as needed.

Exercises and Activities for Entrepreneurial Development

Practical exercises can help you develop key entrepreneurial skills. Role-playing exercises are great for improving your communication and negotiation skills. Practice pitching your business idea to a friend or mentor. This helps you refine your pitch and get comfortable with public speaking.

Networking events are also valuable. Attend local business meetups or join online communities. These events provide opportunities to meet other entrepreneurs, share ideas, and learn from each other. They also help you build a support network that can be invaluable in your entrepreneurial journey.

Daily Practices to Cultivate Entrepreneurial Characteristics

Daily habits can have a big impact on your success. Start your day with a morning routine that includes activities like exercise, reading, and planning your day. Exercise boosts your energy and mood. Reading keeps you informed and inspired. Planning helps you stay focused and organized.

Set aside time each day for reflective thinking. Spend a few minutes reviewing your day. Think about what went well and what could be improved. This practice helps you learn from your experiences and make better decisions.

Mindfulness is another helpful practice. It involves staying present and focused on the moment. This can reduce stress and improve your concentration. Try simple mindfulness exercises like deep breathing or short meditation sessions.

SEEKING FEEDBACK AND MENTORSHIP

Feedback and mentorship are essential for growth. Seek feedback regularly from your peers, employees, and customers. Ask specific questions about your performance and areas for improvement. Listen carefully to their responses and use their feedback to make positive changes.

Find a mentor who has experience in your field. A good mentor can provide guidance, share their experiences, and help you avoid common mistakes. To find a mentor, start by reaching out to people you admire. Attend industry events, join professional groups, and network actively. When you find a potential mentor, approach them respectfully and explain why you value their guidance.

EMBRACING CONTINUOUS LEARNING AND ADAPTABILITY

Successful entrepreneurs never stop learning. Stay curious and open to new experiences. Attend workshops, take online courses, and read books on various topics. This keeps you informed and helps you develop new skills.

Adaptability is also key. The business world is constantly changing. Be ready to pivot when needed. Stay informed about industry trends and be willing to adjust your strategies. This helps you stay competitive and responsive to changes.

Examples of Self-Assessment and Growth

Steve Jobs is a great example of someone who used self-assessment to improve. He was known for his relentless pursuit of excellence. Jobs regularly sought feedback and used it to refine his ideas. His willingness to learn and adapt helped Apple become a leader in innovation.

Another example is Oprah Winfrey. She continuously assessed her strengths and weaknesses. Oprah sought feedback and mentorship throughout her career. Her commitment to self-improvement and adaptability has made her one of the most successful media moguls in the world.

Reed Hastings of Netflix is also noteworthy. He pivoted Netflix from DVD rentals to streaming based on market trends. Hastings used continuous learning to stay ahead in the entertainment industry.

Implementing Practical Exercises in Your Routine

Integrate practical exercises into your daily routine. Start by setting aside time each week for role-playing exercises. Practice pitching your ideas, negotiating deals, and handling tough conversations. This builds your confidence and communication skills.

Attend at least one networking event per month. Whether it's a local meetup or an online webinar, these events provide valuable learning and networking opportunities. Prepare in advance by researching attendees and preparing questions or discussion points.

Create a habit of daily reflection. Spend 10 minutes at the end of each day reviewing your performance. Note what you did well and what you could improve. Use these reflections to make continuous improvements.

DETAILED DAILY PRACTICES FOR ENTREPRENEURS

Develop a structured morning routine. Wake up early and start your day with exercise. This boosts your energy and sets a positive tone for the day. Follow this with 15-30 minutes of reading. Choose books on business, leadership, or personal development.

Plan your day by setting clear priorities. Write down your top three tasks for the day. Focus on completing these tasks before moving on to less important activities. This helps you stay productive and focused.

Practice mindfulness daily. Start with simple exercises like deep breathing or short meditation sessions. Set aside 5-10 minutes each day for mindfulness. This helps reduce stress and improve your concentration.

Seeking Feedback and Finding Mentors

Regularly seek feedback from those around you. Set up regular check-ins with your team to discuss your performance. Ask for honest feedback and be open to criticism. Use this feedback to improve your skills and strategies.

Finding a mentor can greatly accelerate your growth. Look for someone with experience in your field. Reach out to potential mentors with a clear request for guidance. Be respectful of their time and show genuine interest in their advice.

Continuous Learning and Adaptability in Practice

Make learning a daily habit. Dedicate time each day to learning something new. This could be reading an article, taking an online course, or attending a webinar. Continuous learning keeps you informed and adaptable.

Stay adaptable by regularly reviewing your business strategies. Set aside time each month to assess your progress and make necessary adjustments. Be willing to pivot when needed. This keeps you responsive to changes and helps you stay competitive.

Examples of Continuous Learning and Adaptability

Bill Gates is a lifelong learner. Despite his busy schedule, he dedicates time to reading and learning about new topics. This habit has kept him informed and innovative throughout his career.

Sara Blakely, founder of Spanx, continuously adapts her business strategies based on customer feedback. She stays open to new ideas and adjusts her products accordingly. This adaptability has helped her maintain a competitive edge.

Jeff Bezos of Amazon is known for his adaptability. He constantly looks for ways to improve and innovate. Bezos encourages a culture of experimentation at Amazon, which has led to the company's tremendous growth and success.

Building a Flexible Workforce

A flexible workforce is crucial for adaptability. Hire employees who are open to change and willing to learn. Encourage cross-training to develop versatile skills within your team. This ensures your team can handle diverse tasks and adapt to new roles as needed.

Consider flexible work arrangements, such as remote work and flexible hours. These arrangements can improve productivity and job satisfaction. They also help your team adapt to changing circumstances.

Scenario Planning for Preparedness

Scenario planning helps you prepare for different future scenarios. Identify potential challenges and opportunities and develop strategies to address them. This proactive approach helps you stay prepared and adaptable.

Conduct regular scenario planning sessions with your team. Discuss possible future scenarios and how to respond. This helps you anticipate changes and stay ready for any situation.

Encouraging Innovation in Your Business

Innovation drives adaptability. Encourage your team to think creatively and explore new ideas. Create a supportive environment where innovation is valued and rewarded.

Implement innovation programs, such as hackathons or innovation labs. These programs provide opportunities for your team to experiment and develop new solutions. Recognize and reward innovative efforts to motivate your team.

Leveraging Data Analytics for Informed Decisions

Data analytics provides valuable insights for decision-making. Use data to track performance, identify trends, and make informed decisions. This helps you stay proactive and adaptable.

Implement data analytics tools in your business. Platforms like Google Analytics, Tableau, and Power BI provide comprehensive data insights. Use these tools to monitor key metrics and guide your strategies.

Conclusion

Adaptability is a crucial trait for successful entrepreneurs. It involves being flexible, proactive, and open to new technologies. By developing adaptability, you can navigate challenges and seize opportunities.

Start by fostering a culture of flexibility in your business. Stay informed about industry trends and customer feedback. Embrace new technologies and be prepared to pivot when needed.

Learn from successful entrepreneurs who demonstrate adaptability. Follow their examples and see how flexibility, proactive adaptation, and technology integration can benefit your business.

Developing adaptability takes practice and commitment. But the benefits—resilience, innovation, better decision-making, and enhanced customer satisfaction—are well worth the effort.

Embrace adaptability and take your entrepreneurial journey to the next level. Your business will be better prepared to face challenges and seize opportunities, leading to long-term success.

Made in United States
Orlando, FL
23 July 2024

49466423R00090